D1213916

I BELIEVE IN VISIONS

I BELIEVE
IN
VISIONS

Kenneth E. Hagin

FLEMING H. REVELL COMPANY

Old Tappan, New Jersey

Unless otherwise indicated, all Scripture quotations in this volume are from the *King James Version of the Bible*.

Scripture quotations identified as AMPLIFIED are from *The Amplified Bible*. Used by permission of The Lockman Foundation.

Library of Congress Cataloging in Publication Data

Hagin, Kenneth E.   1917–
    I believe in visions.

    1. Visions. 2. Jesus Christ—Apparitions and miracles (Modern) I. Title.
BT580.A1H3   248'.29   72–10332
ISBN 0-8007-0670-6

Contents

I BELIEVE IN VISIONS

1

How God Raised Me From a Deathbed to Preach the Gospel

"He is dead," was the statement made by the doctor who delivered me when I was born prematurely on August 20, 1917, in a house in the 900 block of East Standifer Street in McKinney, Texas. My grandmother, who was present at my birth, tells me that there was no sign of life in me. Thinking I was dead, the doctor laid me on the foot of the bed and he and my grandmother continued to work with my mother, who was in very serious condition. She had been quite ill for several weeks before I was born.

After some forty-five minutes had passed and my mother was doing better, the doctor told my grandmother he would run to his office to get some supplies he needed. While he was gone, my grandmother picked me up to carry me out. Suddenly, she detected a sign of life. She washed me and put a little dress on me, but she had to use a makeshift diaper as the regular kind would have swallowed me. Then she weighed me, and with the little dress and diaper on I weighed slightly more than two pounds; without the clothes, less than two pounds.

Today with our advanced medical knowledge and skill and with the incubators we have to place premature babies in, the chances are practically nil of a baby surviving who weighs less than two pounds. I was born in a day when there were no incubators and I was born in the home, so my chances of living were almost nonexistent.

After awhile the doctor returned, and my grandmother asked him what she should feed the baby. "The baby is dead," he said. "I examined him earlier." When she told him that I was alive and that she had washed and dressed me, he reached into his pocket for a sample package of baby food. "Feed this to him," he said. "It will last longer than he will."

Grandmother mixed the baby food and fed it to me. After that was all gone, she gave me milk, feeding it to me a drop at a time with an eye dropper. She said she had never seen anyone so tiny —that she had a large comb that was no longer than I was. She said that sometimes even a single drop of milk in my mouth would choke me, causing me to strangle and turn blue.

My childhood was not as other children's, for I had been born with a deformed heart and would never be able to lead a normal, active life. I wasn't completely incapacitated, but my activities of necessity had to be limited. I wasn't able to run and play as much as the other children did.

In those days, children didn't start school until the age of seven. However, I learned to read when I was six. My brother was already in school and so I read his books. Since I couldn't use my body, I used my mind.

Soon after I started school I learned that when one is afflicted the other children are prone to take advantage of the weaker child. I guess that proves how big they are. I couldn't fight to defend myself as I would lose my breath, turn blue, and almost pass out. So I decided I would have to have an equalizer.

There was one boy who was the bully of the playground. He was three years older than the rest of us, but had failed three grades and therefore was still in our class. He would run up to someone and knock him or her down. Knowing that I couldn't fight, he seemed to delight in picking on me. One day I found a two-by-four that was about twenty inches long. The next time he hit me, I got that two-by-four, slipped up on him, and knocked him in the head. He was out cold for forty minutes. He soon learned to leave me alone. When one can't fight, he has to learn to take care of himself some way—and I had. My oldest brother learned not to fight with me either, for I knocked him in the head with a hammer one time, and he was unconscious for forty-five minutes.

During the years when I was growing up, I was always very small for my age. My brother would tell me that I would never be any bigger than a fifty-six-year-old man we knew who weighed only eighty-nine pounds and was the size of a ten-year-old boy. When my brother wanted me to do something for him, he would say that if I didn't do it I would turn into a girl when I was twelve years old. Of course, he was always about a half a block away and running when he said that, for he knew I would hit him with anything I could get my hands on.

My father left my mother and us children while I was still very young, leaving her with all the responsibility for providing and caring for us. When I was nine years old I went to live with Mother's parents, as Mother's health was very poor and she needed help in taking care of us.

At the age of fifteen, just four months before my sixteenth birthday, I became totally bedfast. Five doctors were on my case, one of whom had practiced medicine at the Mayo Clinic. My grandfather, although not a wealthy man, was a man of some means. He had quite a bit of property, although this was during the days of the Great Depression when property wasn't worth too much. If the doctors at Mayo Clinic had been able to help me, he would have sent me there. However, our doctors said that the doctor who had been at Mayo was one of the best doctors in

America, and if he said that nothing could be done, it would simply be a waste of time and money to make the trip to the Mayo Clinic. They said there was absolutely no hope for me, that I didn't have one chance in a million of living. As far as medical science was concerned, to their knowledge, no one in my condition had ever lived past sixteen years of age.

Day after day and week after week I lay on the bed of affliction, wondering what was wrong with me. I knew that something was wrong with my heart, but I didn't know exactly what as the doctors didn't tell me. I later learned that I had two serious organic heart problems.

My body became partially paralyzed. I can remember seeing a glass of water beside my bed, wanting to drink it, and not understanding why I couldn't get it. After strict concentration of all my mental powers on it for forty-five minutes, I would be able to reach my hand over to it. But I couldn't pick the glass up. One of the doctors said that I was bordering on total paralysis, and would eventually become completely paralyzed.

There were times when I didn't know anything. Sometimes three weeks would pass in which I would not know anything. My mother and grandmother fed and cared for me, as I was as helpless as a baby. I reached the point where I could hardly hear them talking to me. They later told me that they would put their mouths down to my ear and shout at the top of their voices, but I could barely hear them. It seemed as if they were a block or two away. Then they would put their faces against my face, and I can remember that it was as if I could see them about a block away. I was somewhere between the realm of reality and unreality.

It was on the very first night I became bedfast that I gave my heart to the Lord and was born again—on Saturday, April 22, 1933, at 7:40 P.M. in the south bedroom of 405 North College Street, McKinney, Texas. Earlier that evening my heart stopped beating and the spiritual man that lives in my body departed. When death seized my body, my grandmother, my youngest brother, and my mother sat in the room. I had time only to tell them "goodbye"; then the inward man rushed out of my body and left my body lying dead, with eyes set and flesh cold.

I went down, down, down, until the lights of the earth faded away. I don't mean that I fainted; I don't mean that I was unconscious—I have proof that I was actually dead. My eyes were set, my heart had stopped beating, and my pulse had ceased.

The Scriptures tell about the lost being cast into outer darkness, where there is weeping, wailing, and gnashing of teeth (Matthew 25:30). The further down I went the blacker it became, until it was all blackness. I could not have seen my hand if it had been one inch in front of my eyes. The further down I went, the hotter it was and the more stifling it became.

Finally, far down below me I could see lights flickering on the walls of the caverns of the damned. They were caused by the fires of hell. The giant, white-crested orb of flame pulled me, drawing me as a magnet draws metal to itself. *I did not want to go!* I did not walk, but just as metal jumps to the magnet, my spirit was drawn to that place. I could not take my eyes off it. The heat beat me in the face. Many years have now gone by, yet I can see it as clearly as I saw it then. It is just as fresh in my memory as though it happened last night.

I came to the entrance of hell. Someone might ask, "What does the entrance of hell look like?" I could not describe it, because if I tried I would have to have something with which to compare it. If someone had never seen a tree in his life, it would be impossible to tell him what a tree looked like, as there would be nothing with which to compare it.

Coming to the entrance, I paused. I did not come to a complete halt but just paused momentarily, for I did not want to go. I sensed that one more foot, one more step, one more yard, and I would be forever gone and could not come out of that horrible place.

Upon reaching the bottom of the pit, I became conscious of some kind of spirit being by my side. I had not looked at him because I could not take my gaze off the fires of hell, but, when I paused, that creature laid his hand on my arm to escort me in.

At that same moment a voice spoke from far above the blackness, above the earth, and above the heavens. It was the voice of God. I did not see Him and I do not know what He said because He did not speak in English. He spoke some other tongue. When He spoke it reverberated throughout the region of the damned, shaking it like a leaf in the wind and causing that creature to relax his grip on my arm. I did not turn around, but there was an unseen power that pulled me, and I came away from the fire, away from the heat, back into the shadows of the absorbing darkness.

I began to ascend until I came to the top of the pit and saw the light of the earth. I came back into that room just as real as at any other time I had entered it through the door, with the exception that my spirit needed no doors. I slipped back into my body as a man slips into his trousers in the morning, the same way in which I had gone out—through my mouth.

I began to talk to my grandmother. She said, "Son, I thought you were dead." My great-grandfather had been a medical doctor and she had worked with him. She later told me, "I have dressed many people for burial and laid them out in days gone by. I have had much experience with death, but I learned more about death in dealing with you and your experiences than I ever knew before. You were dead. You had no pulse or heartbeat, and your eyes were set."

"Grandmother," I said, "I didn't go then, but I am going. I am dying! Where is Mother?"

"Your mother is out on the porch," she said, and about that

time I heard my mother praying as she walked up and down the porch.

"Where is my brother?" I asked.

"He ran next door to call the doctor," she replied.

"Grannie, I want to tell Mother goodbye, but I don't want you to leave me. You tell her" I said, and left a message for my mother with her. Then I said, "Grannie, I appreciate you. When Mother's health failed so she could not care for me, you were a second mother to me. Now I am going, and I won't be back this time." I knew I was dying, unprepared to meet God.

My heart stopped beating in my breast again. For the second time, my spirit left my body. I began to descend again into darkness until the lights of earth had faded. Down below, the same experience occurred. God spoke from heaven and again my spirit came out of that place—back into my room and into my body. I began to talk to my grandmother again and then I said, "I will not be back this time, Grandmother." I told her a few more things to tell some of my folks. Then for the third time, I slipped out of my body and began to descend.

I wish I had words adequate to describe the horrors of hell. People go through this life so complacent, so unconcerned, as though they will not have to face hell. But God's Word and my own personal experiences tell me differently. I know what it is to be unconscious, and it is black when you are unconscious. But there is no blackness to compare with the outer darkness.

When I began to descend the third time, my spirit cried out and I literally screamed, "God, I belong to the church. I've been baptized in water." I listened for Him to answer, but no answer came—only my own voice as it came back to mock me.

It will take more than belonging to the church. It will take more than being baptized in water to miss hell and make heaven. Jesus said, ". . . Ye must be born again" (John 3:7). Certainly, I believe in being baptized in water, but only after a person is born again. Certainly, I believe in joining the church and banding together as Christians to work for God. But if you have just joined the church, have just been baptized in water, but haven't been really born again, you will go to hell.

As I came out of that pit the third time, my spirit began to pray. My physical voice picked up the prayer, right where my spirit had been praying. I prayed so loudly that neighbors could hear me. People started coming to the house to see what had happened because they heard my praying and heard my mother as she walked the porch and prayed at the top of her voice. I looked at the clock and saw that it was twenty minutes before eight o'clock. That was the very hour I was born again due to the mercy of God, through the prevailing prayers of my mother.

My prayer was not depending upon church membership or water baptism, but as I began to call upon God my prayer was that He would have mercy on me, a sinner, and that He would forgive me for my sins and cleanse me from all unrighteousness. I accepted Him, confessed Him, and took Him as my Saviour. I felt so wonderful, as if a heavy burden had rolled off my chest.

Although I was rejoicing and happy in my spirit, although I felt wonderful spiritually, I felt no better physically. The doctors had been called and they told my folks that I was going to die. I thought I would die that night. But this thought no longer bothered me. I knew that I was ready to go then.

My experience of being brought back from the dead is not new. Jesus raised Lazarus from the dead, as well as Jairus' daughter and the widow's son. The Apostle Peter raised Dorcas from the dead; the Apostle Paul raised a young man from the dead—others down through church history have had similar experiences.

Through my experience, God brought me to a knowledge of salvation, and that is the best thing in the world to know. I was so thankful to know that my heart was right with God, that if I should die before morning I would go to be with Him. Every night when the lights were out and my family was in bed, I was left alone with my thoughts, and I did a lot of thinking and praying. I remember thanking God that I was saved and was His child. I told the Lord that I was going to go to sleep smiling and praising Him, and that if I should die during the night they would find me the next morning with a smile on my face. If I left this life, I would go with a praise in my heart. While praising the Lord, I drifted off to sleep. I never had to take anything to help me sleep. And this still works today. The Bible tells us that God ". . . giveth his beloved sleep" (Psalms 127:2). I am His beloved, as is every Christian; so we can simply take that verse, thank Him for it, and go peacefully to sleep. We don't need any tranquilizers.

The next morning when I awakened with the sun streaming across my bed, the first thing I did was to praise God. I would thank Him for the light of another day. I would thank Him for the sun, the trees and flowers, the grass and the leaves. I would thank God for the songs that the birds sang. I praised Him for all of these little things that are so wonderful, marvelous, and beautiful. I had never heard anyone praise God before this, but when one's heart is in tune with God and he knows he is ready for heaven, there is an automatic praise in his soul. I didn't know anything about divine healing. I didn't know that God answered that kind of prayer. But I thanked God that I didn't die and go to hell.

At noon, my grandmother would bring my lunch to me on a tray. I would pray and thank God for the food, and then I would say, "Lord, I guess I won't be here by the time the evening shadows fall. I'll probably slip away this afternoon. But I'm so glad I am saved. I am so glad You didn't let me die and go to hell. I am so glad I didn't have to stay down there."

After awhile evening came and soon I would be alone in the dark again. I would again praise the Lord for salvation and would tell Him that probably I would pass away during the night, but that I was thankful to be saved and to be ready to meet Him. Then I would go to sleep smiling and praising the Lord. Day after day, week after week, and month after month I did this.

In the fall of that year when the weather became cooler, I began to feel somewhat better. Grandmother would prop me up in bed. Then she would bring her Bible to me and prop it up in front of me. I often tell folks that I was a Baptist boy reading my grandmother's Methodist Bible.

When I first started reading the Bible, I could read only ten minutes at a time—I couldn't see after that—then that was all for the day. The next day I would read for another ten or fifteen minutes. After a few weeks of reading in this way, I could read for an hour at a time. Finally, I could read for as long as I liked.

I had been brought up in Sunday school. I can't remember the first time I went to church. It seemed that I had prayed all my life. Nor can I remember the first time I ever read the Bible. But until that Saturday night, April 22, when God permitted me to have a glimpse into hell, I had never really been born again. You can be religious and not really be a born-again child of God. When you are born again, however, the very same Bible that you have been reading all your life suddenly looks different. As I read Grandmother's Bible, I found that Jesus Christ is the same yesterday, today, and forever.

The doctors had said that I could die at any time, so when I began reading the Bible I began with the New Testament. I reasoned, "I might not be alive ten minutes from now, so I will utilize this ten minutes, or whatever time I have, and will start with the New Testament."

I read through the Book of Matthew and began reading the Book of Mark. I read a verse which was to transform my life.

"Therefore I say unto you, What things soever ye desire, when ye pray, believe that ye receive them, and ye shall have them" (Mark 11:24).

Salvation is, of course, the most important thing that can happen to a person. But you cannot possibly understand the all-consuming desire a person can have for health, healing, and life when he has never had a normal childhood, has been sick all of his life, and then lies bedfast month after month, knowing that this will be his deathbed before long.

The greatest desire of my heart was to be well and strong. And here in this verse of Scripture Jesus said, ". . . What things soever ye desire, when ye pray, believe that ye receive them, and ye shall have them." It seemed as if someone had turned on a bright light in a very dark room. And you cannot imagine how dark it can be, even in the daytime, when you are shut in between four walls and are staring at the ceiling all the time with a feeling of utter hopelessness.

I didn't know that the Psalmist had said, "Thy word is a lamp unto my feet, and a light unto my path" (Psalms 119:105). But without knowing the Word, I had the experience. The whole room seemed suddenly engulfed in light, and there seemed to be light on the inside of me. I have never forgotten that experience or that Scripture. Since then it is as if it had been branded on my heart.

Naturally, the devil was right there to plant doubt in my heart. The minute the light came, he came, too. I didn't know at the time, however, that it was the devil. I didn't have enough spiritual discernment or knowledge of the Word to know.

Subtly the thought came that maybe the words, ". . . what things soever ye desire," didn't apply to physical things but just to spiritual things. Maybe it just meant, ". . . what things soever ye desire" spiritually. Then the light went out. Doubt had blown out the candle of faith, and I was in the dark again. I had believed what the devil told me, and again I thought there was no hope. I had to die!

I decided to send for my pastor and ask him exactly what Mark 11:24 meant. Looking back now I see how foolish it was to have to send for someone to ask if Jesus really told the truth or not. But this was all so new to me, and I had great confidence in my pastor up until this time. I would have believed anything he told me. I was just like so many other people who are following men and not really following God.

I try to tell people to whom I minister not to believe something just because I say it. That doesn't make it so. If I cannot prove by the Bible that what I am saying is truth, then don't believe it. Don't accept it. I have no right to force any of my theories or pet doctrines on someone else. I would not want to impose any of my convictions on others. Let us live by the Word.

Longing to talk to my pastor about this Scripture, I called my grandmother to my bedside and asked her to go get the pastor, who lived about four blocks from our house. She walked to the parsonage and asked to see the pastor. She told him that I wanted him to come to see me. He said that he was very busy that day, but that he would come two days later. She suggested that he come early in the morning, because I was more rested then and more alert than I was later in the day. After about ten o'clock in the morning I lay in a stupor for the rest of the day. He said that he would come about eight-thirty in the morning.

During the years before I became bedfast, I had been very faithful in attending Sunday school. I never missed. Yet in all the time I had been sick, he had not been to see me once. When Thursday morning came, the day appointed for his visit, I eagerly looked forward to seeing him and asking him the questions that burned on my heart. Eight-thirty came and went. Nine o'clock came, and anxiously I looked for my pastor. Nine-thirty, then ten o'clock, but still no word from him. And even though I lay on that bed for another entire year, he never did come to see me.

Although I was crushed with disappointment and disillusionment at the time, I could look back later and see that it was best that he did not come, for he would have told me the wrong thing. Rather than inspiring my faith to believe God for my physical healing, he would have simply reinforced the doubts I already had.

When my pastor didn't come to see me, my grandmother walked to another part of town to see another preacher in whom she had great confidence. She told him about my condition, and that I had asked to see a preacher. He told her that he would come, but he, too, failed to keep his promise. Although again I cried with disappointment when he did not arrive, it was really a blessing that he didn't. It was like many things that we cry about, but which are for our own good and we don't realize it at the time. We wouldn't be crying if we could just see into the future.

My aunt, who was a member of another church, said that her pastor would come to see me. However, by this time I was certain that he, too, would not come. My aunt was superintendent of the Junior Department in the Sunday school of her church, and during the years that I was eligible to go in her department, when I was nine through eleven years of age, I went to Sunday school with her. I had met her pastor, of course, and during that time I never missed a Sunday.

As I said, even though this pastor had promised to visit me, by this time I was rather skeptical and didn't really expect him. One day I heard someone knocking on the front door. A member of my family answered the door, and the minute I heard the voice of the caller I recognized it as the voice of this pastor. Suddenly my heart leaped with joy because I thought I could ask him what this Scripture meant. Surely, he would know and could clear up this confusion in my mind. I knew that if this

Scripture meant what I thought it meant, then I was coming out of that bed.

At that time only one person at a time was allowed in my room, so he came in alone. No one in my family could come in with him. I couldn't see him too clearly until he stooped over me. Then his face came into focus. Partially paralyzed in my throat and tongue, I could not speak distinctly, and I would say a lot of things backwards. It sometimes would take me a long time to get some things out. My brain didn't seem to work right. I often would have to stumble around for ten minutes before I could ask a question.

I was moving my mouth and lips trying to say something. I tried to call his name, and I tried to tell him to get my Bible and turn to Mark 11:24 and tell me what it meant, but I couldn't get the words out. I was just stuttering; I couldn't frame the words. Before I could say anything, he thought that I just couldn't talk. He patted my hand and said in his professionally pious voice, "Just be patient, my boy, and in a few more days it will all be over." Then he laid my hand down and left the room.

The despair that descended upon me in that moment is beyond words! There was no need for me to ask him what I wanted to know. I had my answer. If he had thought there were any hope for me, he would have told me so. If he had known what that verse of Scripture meant, and that it held anything for me, he would have told me. But he left me alone—without faith, and without hope.

Although this pastor had prayed no prayer with me, he went into the living room and said a prayer with my family sitting there. For some reason my hearing was very keen at this time, and I could hear distinctly every word he said, although he didn't pray very loudly. He said, "Heavenly Father, we ask you to bless this dear grandmother and grandfather that are about to be bereaved of this grandson. Prepare their hearts for this dark hour that is about to come upon them."

As I listened to his prayer, I was like the naughty little boy who was being punished by his schoolteacher by having to stand in the corner with his nose in a circle that she had drawn on the blackboard. He might have been standing up outwardly, but he thought to himself that on the inside he was sitting down. I felt just as rebellious as that little boy. Although I couldn't speak the words audibly, on the inside of me I was shouting, "I'm not dead yet!"

I listened as this pastor continued his prayer. "Bless this dear brokenhearted mother who is about to lose her son." My mother had had some hope up until then, but he robbed her of what she had and she started crying.

After the preacher left, my grandmother came into my room and asked me if it would be all right for this preacher to preach my funeral as he was the only one who had come to see me. I agreed that this would be all right. Then she asked me what songs I wanted sung at my funeral. I told her that I didn't have any favorites, that they could sing whatever they wanted. She suggested two or three, and I said they would be all right. Then she asked me about pallbearers. She suggested some men, and I told her that they would be all right. My mother asked me if I wanted to be buried in a certain place that she mentioned, and I agreed. Then they left my room. Although the sun was still shining brightly outside, it seemed ever so dark in my room.

All of this so stunned me that I lay on my bed for the next thirty days without moving. I gave up and just waited to die. After about thirty days, I began to read the Bible again. I couldn't seem to get away from the following verse: "What things soever ye desire, when ye pray, believe that ye receive them, and ye shall have them" (Mark 11:24).

Later in the fall I became bolder. I told the Lord that I had sent for two preachers who didn't come. The third one came, but I realized that it would have been better if he hadn't. I told the Lord that when He was on earth He said, "What things soever ye desire, when ye pray, believe that ye receive them, and ye shall have them," and that I desired to be healed. I told Him that I was going to take Him at His Word. I was going to believe that He told the truth, and that this verse meant what it said. If the New Testament was true, then I was going to come off this bed. I told Him that I was going to live and not die. "If I don't get off of this bed, then the Bible isn't so, and I am going to have them take it and throw it in the trash can." I meant business!

I was determined to get up from that bed, but I still didn't know how to act my faith in that verse of Scripture. A person can cry and pray and do everything he knows to do, but if he doesn't have faith, he will remain the same. Jesus didn't say just to pray. The key word in this Scripture is *believe.*

At this time, I didn't fully understand faith. I prayed and prayed, but I didn't get any results. I was sure that God heard me, and I had a good feeling inside me. Yet my heart still wasn't beating normally. What I didn't know then is that we have to go by faith, not by our feelings. We have to stand on the promises in God's Word, and not look at the circumstances surrounding us.

I did improve to the extent that I was able to use my hands. My grandmother would sometimes prop me up in bed for a short time. I reached down and felt my leg. There was no muscle at all, just bone. I was extremely skinny.

I seemed to be making no real headway, however, and I said, "Lord, I thought You would heal me." I was so sure that He had heard me, but I felt no better. I know now that just because you feel better after you pray, that is no sign that God heard you. Or just because you feel no better after you pray, that is no sign that God didn't hear you. We cannot rely on how we feel. We have to come back to what God's Word says about the matter. For months I struggled along in this way.

When New Year's Day, 1934, rolled around, it was moving day. Grandfather owned several houses in town, and he decided to move into another one of them. He had told the people who were renting this certain house that he wanted it for his own use. When they moved, he had it redecorated and we were ready to move in. When the movers came, they moved the furniture from the other parts of the house first, saving the furniture in my bedroom until the last. When they came to move my furniture, an ambulance came and moved me.

While I was riding along in the ambulance, one of the attendants remarked that he had heard I had been in bed for about a year now. "Nine months, to be exact," I told him. He then said that if I felt like it, they would take me for a little ride through the residential areas so I could see the scenery. I was so happy for this chance to see things I had been missing for so many months now. The smallest joys, which we so often take for granted, can bring immense pleasure to one who has been deprived of them for so long.

I was able to move my head to look out the window as they drove slowly through the town. Then the ambulance attendant said, "Son, if you feel up to it, we'll drive down to the square. Since it is a holiday, there probably won't be much traffic and you might enjoy it." How wonderful, I thought, to get to see that old courthouse again, the stores, and other buildings in this beloved little town of McKinney with its population of eight or nine thousand.

I saw the familiar old drugstore on the corner. I saw the J. C. Penney's store. Next to that was the Mode O'Day dress shop and next to that was Woolworth's. On down was a shoe store and on the next corner a ladies' ready-to-wear shop. Then we went down the west side of the square and turned to go down the south side. I drank in all of these sights, not knowing when, if ever, I might see them again.

Just as we turned the corner and started down the south side of the square, I turned and looked at the old courthouse that sat in the middle of the square. I shall never forget that moment as long as I live. In that instant something said to me, "Well, you never did think you would ever see these old buildings again. And you wouldn't have if it hadn't been for the kindness of the man who is taking you."

Then I remembered the verse in Mark 11:24: "What things soever ye desire, when ye pray, believe that ye receive them, and ye shall have them," and I recalled the verse that went before it which said, ". . . he shall have whatsoever he saith" (verse 23). Here is the principle of faith: believe in your heart, say it with your mouth, and "he shall have whatsoever he saith."

As I said it in that ambulance that day, tears rolled down my face. I didn't understand all that I know now. I had just one small gleam of light. It was like a little light that might peep through a crack in a door, but it was a beginning point for me—this first day of January, 1934, about two o'clock in the afternoon.

I said, "Yes, I will see these buildings and this courthouse. I will come and stand in this courthouse square, because Jesus said that what you believe in your heart and say with your mouth shall come to pass." I had committed myself.

January and February went by, and I was still bedfast. March, April, May, June, and July went by. The devil might have said it wasn't working, but I held on to my confession and refused to give up. I kept telling the Lord that I was going to hold on, that I was standing on His Word, and it had to work!

Finally, I saw what I had been doing wrong. I saw that I wasn't really believing what God's Word said. I was saying it in my mind, but I wasn't believing it with my heart or acting upon it with my heart. I saw that for months I had been hoping that I would grow better, gradually. I was praying with hope and not with faith, and that won't get the job done. I realized that my faith was not based on what God's Word said, but on what I could see and feel. I could feel that my heart wasn't beating right yet. I would often look at my legs and arms and start crying. I could see that they were unchanged. I was believing only what I could see with my physical eyes.

Thus I came to the second week of August, 1934. On Tuesday morning, I prayed through the early morning hours. At the usual time my mother came in and helped me with my bath. It was about eight-thirty when she left the room; I continued to pray. I had been struggling with that verse in Mark 11:24 for a long time now, but I still wasn't any better. I told the Lord, "You said when You were on earth that 'what things soever ye desire, when ye pray, believe that ye receive them, and ye shall have them.' I desire to be healed and I believe. If You were to stand here in my room and I could see You with my physical eyes and take hold of Your hand, and if You were to tell me that my trouble is that I am not believing, I would have to say that this isn't true. I am believing."

Then a voice on the inside of me spoke so clearly, it was as real to me as if someone had spoken audibly. "Yes, you are believing as far as you know, but the last clause of that verse says, 'and ye shall have them.'"

I believed as much as I knew how to believe, but I didn't know enough. A person cannot pray and get faith. The Bible says that faith comes ". . . by hearing, and hearing by the word of God" (Romans 10:17). We need knowledge of the Word. When this light of knowledge from the Word comes, faith is automatically there.

In this moment, I saw exactly what that verse in Mark 11:24 meant. Until then I was going to wait till I was actually healed.

I was looking at my body and testing my heartbeat to see if I had been healed. But I saw that the verse says that you have to believe when you pray. The *having* comes after the *believing*. I had been reversing it. I was trying to *have* first and then *believe* second. And that is what most folks do.

"I see it. I see it," I said with joy. "I see what I've got to do, Lord. I've got to believe that my heart is well while I'm still lying here on this bed, and while my heart is not beating right. I've got to believe that my paralysis is gone while I'm still lying here flat on my back and helpless.

"I believe in my heart that You have heard my prayer. I believe that my heart is healed and that my paralysis is gone. I believe in my heart that I have received healing for my body."

As I said this the thought came to me—*You're a pretty thing! Just look at you, claiming to be a Christian and here you are lying. Don't you know that the Bible says that all liars will have their part in the lake that burneth with fire and brimstone?*

"I am not a liar," I declared.

"Certainly you are, because you said that you are healed and you're not."

"I didn't say that I am healed because I feel like it," I stated. "I'm healed because I believe it. And, devil, if you say that I am not, then you are a liar. I am acting on the Word of God. If I am not healed, then Jesus is a liar. Go argue with God about it, don't fuss with me."

With this, the devil left me alone. Then I said, "Thank God, I'm healed." I lifted my hands and praised God. Momentarily, I started to feel my heart to see if it was beating normally, but I caught myself and stated that I wasn't going by feelings but by faith. I kept saying that my heart was well. I praised the Lord in this manner for about ten minutes.

Then the Holy Spirit spoke as an inner witness on the inside of me and said, "You believe that you are healed. If you are healed, then you should be up and out of that bed."

I felt this was right, so I pushed myself up to a sitting position with my hands. Then I reached down, got hold of my feet, and swung them around to the side of the bed. I couldn't feel them, but I could see them. Then I said that I was going to stand and walk. The devil fought me every inch of the way. He kept telling me that I was a fool. Of course I couldn't walk, he would tell me. As long as the devil can keep us in the sense realm, he will defeat us. But if we will stay in the faith realm, we will defeat him!

I got hold of the bedpost and pulled myself up. The room started spinning, for I had been in this bed for sixteen months. I closed my eyes, wrapped my arm around the bedpost, and stood there for a few minutes. Finally I opened my eyes and everything had stopped spinning.

I declared that I was healed and that I was going to walk. Feeling began to return to my legs, and it seemed as though two million pins were pricking me. The nerves were being reactivated. I was rejoicing because it was so wonderful to have feeling back in those lifeless legs, in spite of the painful prickling sensation. After a short time, the pain left and I felt normal.

Determined now more than ever to walk, I held on to the bedpost and cautiously took a step. Then I took another. Holding on to pieces of furniture, I managed to walk around the room one time.

I told no one of this, but the next morning I got up and did the same thing. That night I asked my mother to bring me some clothes as I was going to get up and go to the breakfast table the next morning. She was shocked, but she did as I asked. On the third morning I got out of bed, dressed myself, walked into the kitchen, and joined my family at the breakfast table. And I've been doing it ever since.

On the second Saturday of August, 1934, I walked to the courthouse square. It was crowded downtown as people always came to town on Saturday to do their shopping, so I had to elbow my way through the crowd to get to the outside curb of the square. As I stood there, tears coursed down my face and I thanked God for His goodness. I took out my New Testament which I had brought along with me, and I don't know what people thought as they watched me standing on the corner with tears streaming down my face as I opened the New Testament to read, but I didn't care. I had read the Scripture which says, "Prove all things; hold fast that which is good" (1 Thessalonians 5:21). I had proved the verse in Mark 11:24, which I had come to love, and had found it true in my life. I knew that God's Word was true. It was possible to have "what things soever ye desire" by right believing in God's Word.

Some time later, a doctor checked my heart and said that I no longer had any kind of heart trouble. He said that people with the type of heart condition that I had almost never get well. This had to be a real miracle, for now he could find nothing wrong with me.

I soon began my ministry as a young Baptist preacher, and pastored a community church just eight miles from that courthouse square. The first year that I pastored, I wore out four pairs of shoes walking to preach. I walked down dusty old roads to preach the gospel, to tell of how Jesus had saved me and had healed me. I used to say, "I'll preach from the Red River to the Gulf of Mexico, telling everywhere I go that Jesus saves, heals, and is coming again. And I'll preach it from the Louisiana border to the New Mexico state line." I thought, at that time, that would be covering quite a bit of territory.

Because I believed in divine healing, I began associating with the Full Gospel people who also believed and preached about divine healing. I liked to go to their services, because it was just like getting a shot in the arm and it made my faith grow stronger. They also preached about being filled with the Holy Ghost and speaking in other tongues—something I didn't quite understand or altogether agree with. But I tolerated this in order to have fellowship on the subject of divine healing.

I wasn't accustomed to services in which everyone would pray at once, and this nearly worried me to death at first. I started to say something a time or two to straighten these people out. Then I heard someone else tell them, "Don't you know that God is not hard of hearing?"

"He is not nervous either," they replied.

When they invited Christians to come and pray at the altar, I would go forward to pray with them. But I would get as far away as I could because their praying all at once bothered me. I would get off in a corner somewhere and pray quietly.

After awhile the thought occurred to me that these folks knew about divine healing and my church apparently didn't. They might know something more here than I did. I decided to go through the Acts of the Apostles to see how the early church prayed. As I read, I couldn't find one place where they called on Deacon Brown or Sister Jones to lead in prayer. I found to my utter amazement that in the early church everyone prayed at once. "And being let go, they went to their own company, and reported all that the chief priests and elders had said unto them. And when they heard that, they lifted up their voice to God with one accord . . ." (Acts 4:23, 24).

The thing that clinched it with me was the sixteenth chapter of Acts where I read that Paul and Silas were in jail at midnight. Their backs were bleeding. Their feet were in stocks. Yet at midnight they prayed and sang praises to God. ". . . and the prisoners heard them" (Acts 16:25). Up until then I had believed in praying to God, but I believed in being quiet about it. But here I saw that Paul and Silas weren't quiet even in jail.

The next time I went to the Full Gospel service and they invited everyone to the altar to pray, I got right in the middle of them and lifted my voice just as they did. I felt wonderful release and freedom in prayer. The Word of God will set you free. Jesus said, "And ye shall know the truth, and the truth shall make you free" (John 8:32). God's Word is truth, and it will set you free.

But the subject of the baptism of the Holy Ghost and speaking with other tongues which these Full Gospel folks preached was quite another matter. That "tongues" business—that was a bitter pill to swallow. I had been warned against that. But as one fellow down in East Texas had said about going around with these Full Gospel people, "It is like a slippery creek bank. You keep fooling around and you'll slip in."

I meditated and thought on the Scriptures concerning the Holy Spirit and came to the conclusion that these Full Gospel folks were wrong. Tongues weren't necessary; they weren't for us today. A believer could receive this enduement of power without speaking in tongues. That was my own judgment, of course. It certainly wasn't Scripture.

I said to the Lord, "These folks are good people, I know. They are thoroughly saved, born again, and they knew about divine healing when my church didn't. I certainly do believe in the Holy Ghost. And I believe in the infilling, the enduement of power from on high. I sense a lack of power in my own life, and I know I need the infilling of the Holy Ghost. And I expect to receive all right. But I am of the opinion that the tongues don't go along with it and are not for us today."

Immediately the Lord spoke to my heart. I knew that it was the Holy Spirit speaking through the Word. That same still small voice that had brought me off a bed of affliction and into divine healing asked me, "What does the Bible say?"

I quoted the Scripture, "For the promise is unto you, and to your children, and to all that are afar off, even as many as the Lord our God shall call" (Acts 2:39).

Then the voice said, "What promise is that?"

". . . and ye shall receive the gift of the Holy Ghost" (Acts 2:38). "The reference here, Lord, is to the promise of the gift of the Holy Ghost." Then I hastened to add, "But Lord, I believe in the Holy Ghost. It is the tongues I am not sure about."

The Holy Spirit always leads us in line with the Word. The Word and the Spirit agree. I am not in favor of just following voices, for a person can go wrong following voices. But we can never go wrong following any voice that leads us to walk in line with the Word of God. Jesus said, "He shall receive of mine, and shall shew it unto you" (John 16:14). And, "He shall not speak of himself" (verse 13). Thank God, He does speak. "But whatsoever he shall hear, that shall he speak" (verse 13).

The born-again Christian has the Holy Ghost in a measure; however, this is not the same as an enduement of power. He is not filled with the Holy Ghost. But there is the work of the Holy Spirit in the new birth. "The Spirit itself beareth witness with our spirit, that we are the children of God" (Romans 8:16).

Then the Lord said to me, "What does Acts 2:4 say?"

I could quote the Scripture, of course. But just because you have it in your head does not mean that you really know what it says. You have to have the revelation of it in your spirit to really know what the Word of God means.

I quoted, "And they were all filled with the Holy Ghost, and began to speak with other tongues, as the Spirit gave them utterance." I got this far and said, " 'And they were all filled with the Holy Ghost, and began to sp . . .' Oh, I see it, I see it. 'They were all filled with the Holy Ghost, and began to speak.' When I get filled with the Holy Ghost, I will begin to speak in other tongues. Lord, that settles it. I am going down right now to the Full Gospel preacher's house and receive the Holy Ghost."

I walked over to the parsonage and knocked on the door. I said, "I've come to get the Holy Ghost."

He said, "Wait." From that day until this I have never been able to figure out why anyone would ever tell someone to wait to get the Holy Ghost. Someone said, "Didn't you read where Jesus told the disciples to tarry, and 'to tarry' means 'to wait'?" Yes, but that is not a formula for receiving the Holy Ghost. If that were a formula for receiving the Holy Ghost, then why take out the word *Jerusalem?* Jesus said, ". . . tarry ye in the city of Jerusalem, until ye be endued with power from on high" (Luke 24:49). It was just as necessary for that group—the one hundred and twenty—to be in Jerusalem as it was that they wait.

Also, they weren't waiting—getting ready and preparing themselves—to be filled with the Holy Ghost. They were waiting for the day of Pentecost. The Holy Ghost could not be given until then. If they had been waiting and preparing themselves, the Bible would have read, "When they were ready . . ." But it reads, "And when the day of Pentecost was fully come . . ." (Acts 2:1).

Someone said, "Well, waiting gets you ready." No, it doesn't. Getting saved gets you ready. A fellow down in East Texas said, "I had to take back a pig I had stolen before I could get the Holy Ghost."

I said, "I had to do that to get saved."

This is trying to clean yourself up. But you can't clean yourself up. ". . . the blood of Jesus Christ his Son cleanseth us from all sin" (1 John 1:7). If you are bloodwashed, you are ready right now.

Cornelius and his household were not only saved but were also filled with the Holy Ghost almost in the same instant (Acts 11:14, 15). They didn't have time to get ready. The Holy Ghost fell upon them, and they began to speak with tongues. If it hadn't been for speaking with tongues, we Gentiles never would have gotten in the church. It was strictly a Jewish church up until then. Even Peter himself didn't know that the Gentiles could be saved until he had the vision which is recorded in the first part of the tenth chapter of Acts. It astonished the Jews who came with Peter when the Holy Ghost was poured out on the Gentiles. "For they heard them speak with tongues, and magnify God . . ." (Acts 10:46).

When I told the Full Gospel pastor, "I have come here to get the Holy Ghost," and he told me to wait, I blurted out, "But it won't take me long to receive." As the church was having a revival service that night and it was then already six o'clock in the evening, he wanted me to wait and seek for the baptism in the service. But I knew I would have to wait until seven-thirty when the service started. Then I would have to wait until the preliminaries were over, and then the preaching. It would have been nine o'clock before I could have gotten to the altar. But why wait for a gift?

I have been associated with Full Gospel folks for many years, and in all that time I have never told anyone to wait. If people say they want to get saved tonight, you don't say, "Wait and come to church Sunday and seek for it." If someone wanted you to pray for their healing, you wouldn't say, "Wait." They want to get healed right now, especially if they are in pain. Salvation is a gift, healing is a gift, and so is the Holy Ghost.

Seeing my eagerness as I said, "It won't take me long to receive," the pastor reluctantly said, "Well, come on in then." Another pastor said, "I know you can receive the Holy Ghost right away because we read about it in the Acts of the Apostles. But when you have to wait a long time, the experience means so much more to you. Take me for instance. It took me three years and six months to get the Holy Ghost. I waited and I waited, I tarried and I sought. Now the Holy Ghost really means something to me."

I said, "Well, poor old Paul didn't know that. I wish you could have gotten to him and told him about it. He didn't know that and he got the Holy Ghost immediately when Ananias laid hands on him. He didn't wait or tarry or seek. But then, all he ever did was to write half of the New Testament. Of course, he did more singlehandedly in thirty-eight years of his ministry than any denomination has done in five hundred years put together. But if you could have gotten to him and told him to wait for three years and six months, then maybe the Holy Ghost would have meant something to him."

I went into the living room and knelt down before a large chair. I closed out everything around me, shut my eyes, and lifted my hands. No one told me to do it, but I just lifted my hands. I said, "Dear Lord, I have come here to receive the Holy Ghost." I repeated in my prayer what I had just learned from Acts 2:39 and Acts 2:4. Then I said, "Your Word says that the Holy Ghost is a gift. Therefore, I realize that the Holy Spirit is received by faith. I received the gift of salvation by faith. I received healing for my body by faith. Now I receive the gift that You offer."

Let me point out here that the Holy Spirit was given on the day of Pentecost, and that He has been here ever since. God hasn't given Him to anyone since the day of Pentecost. It is just a matter now of folks receiving Him. I can't find in the Acts of the Apostles where the disciples ever asked anyone, "Has God given you the Holy Ghost?" But I do read where they asked, "Have you received?" The emphasis is not on God's giving, because He has already done that. The emphasis is on man's receiving.

In the Scripture, the Word says, "Therefore being by the right hand of God exalted, and having received of the Father the promise of the Holy Ghost, [Jesus received of the Father the promise of the Holy Ghost. After He received the promise of the Holy Ghost] he hath shed forth this, which ye now see and hear" (Acts 2:33).

". . . Paul having passed through the upper coasts came to Ephesus: and finding certain disciples" (Acts 19:1). Paul didn't ask them, "Has God given you the Holy Ghost?" He said, "Have ye received the Holy Ghost since ye believed" (Acts 19:2)?

"Now when the apostles which were at Jerusalem heard that Samaria had received the word of God, they sent unto them Peter and John: Who, when they were come down, prayed for them, that they might receive the Holy Ghost" (Acts 8:14, 15). Notice that it says, "that they might receive." Peter and John didn't pray that God would give the people in Samaria the Holy Ghost. They didn't even pray that God would pour out the Holy Ghost on them. They prayed that they might receive the Holy Ghost. "Then laid they their hands on them, and they received the Holy Ghost" (Acts 8:17).

"And Ananias went his way, and entered into the house; and putting his hands on him said, Brother Saul, the Lord, even Jesus, that appeared unto thee in the way as thou camest, hath sent me, that thou mightest receive thy sight, and be filled with the Holy Ghost" (Acts 9:17). He didn't say, "God has sent me to pray for you that He would give you the Holy Ghost." He didn't say, "God has sent me to pray for you that He would pour His Holy Ghost out upon you." Ananias said, "He sent me, that thou mightest . . . be filled."

We don't pray that God would send salvation and save someone. All that person has to do is to receive. We don't pray that God would send healing and heal someone, we pray for him that he would receive. Neither do we need to pray that God will send His Spirit to fill a hungry heart. We only need to open our hearts and receive.

There in that parsonage in April, 1937, I said to the Lord, "The Holy Ghost is a gift. I received salvation by faith. I received healing for my body three years ago by faith. Now I receive the gift of the Holy Ghost by faith. And I want to thank You now because I have received."

Notice that we don't speak in tongues, and then know we have the Holy Ghost. We have the Holy Ghost first, then speak in tongues. "And they were all filled with the Holy Ghost [If we stop reading there, we would all know that they are filled. But continuing we read] and began to speak with other tongues, as the Spirit gave them utterance" (Acts 2:4). The speaking with other tongues was a result of having received the Holy Ghost. We receive the Holy Ghost first.

I said to the Lord, "I have received the Holy Ghost. He is in me because Jesus promised that He shall be in You. I say it with my mouth because I believe in my heart that I have received the Holy Ghost. Now I expect to speak with tongues because they did on the day of Pentecost. And thank God, I will. I have received the Holy Ghost, I believe that. And I will speak with tongues now as the Holy Ghost gives me utterance."

After I had prayed that, because I was grateful for the Holy Ghost that I had received, and for the speaking with tongues that He was going to give me, I said, "Hallelujah, Hallelujah." But I had never felt so dry in my life saying it. Feelings and faith are far removed from each other, however, and sometimes when you feel as if you have the least faith, that is when you have the most. So I said, "Hallelujah," about seven or eight times, even though it seemed as if that word would choke me.

About the time I had said "Hallelujah" for the eighth time—not fast, but very slowly—way down inside of me were these strange words. It seemed as if they were just going around inside me. It seemed that I would know what they would sound like if they were spoken, so I just started speaking them out. And eight minutes after I first knocked on that pastor's door, I was speaking with tongues. They had said, "Wait," but instead of waiting, I spent that hour and a half speaking in tongues. It is much better to wait with the Holy Ghost than without.

I believe in waiting on God, of course. We should have tarrying meetings for everyone that is spirit-filled. It is more wonderful to tarry and wait filled with the Holy Ghost than it is without.

During the hour and a half that I was talking in tongues, I had a glorious time in the Lord. Talking in tongues edifies you. "He that speaketh in an unknown tongue edifieth himself . . ." (1 Corinthians 14:4). This is a spiritual edification, or building up. Language students tell us that we have a word in our modern vernacular that is closer to the meaning of the Greek word than "edify" and that is the word "charge." We charge a battery —we build it up. Paul said, "He that speaketh in an unknown tongue edifieth himself." He charges himself. He builds himself up like a battery.

I continued to preach the same thing I had been preaching. I just added a little bit to it. The Holy Ghost will help a minister to enlarge his vision. I said, "I'll preach that Jesus saves and heals. I'll preach that He fills with the Holy Ghost and that He is coming again. And now I'll preach from the Atlantic Coast to the Pacific Coast. (I even got bigger in my thinking than Texas. The Holy Ghost will make you even bigger than Texas.) I'll preach it from Los Angeles to New York. I'll preach it from the Gulf of Mexico to the Canadian border."

And God has blessed my ministry so that I have been able to do it. I have traveled over a million miles throughout the United States and Canada in my automobile. For over thirty years now I have been going throughout the land proclaiming the glorious gospel of our Lord Jesus Christ.

2

Come Up Hither

As the Lord continued to deal with my life, He appeared to me in vision form on several occasions. To understand the Scriptural background for visions, let us go back to the day of Pentecost when Peter stood and boldly preached a sermon to those who were gathered around, amazed at the marvel of the one hundred and twenty men and women who were speaking in other tongues following the mighty outpouring of the Holy Ghost. A portion of Peter's message to the crowd is found in the second chapter of the Book of Acts.

"But Peter, standing up with the eleven, lifted up his voice, and said unto them, Ye men of Judea, and all ye that dwell at Jerusalem, be this known unto you, and hearken to my words: For these are not drunken, as ye suppose, seeing it is but the third hour of the day. But this is that which was spoken by the prophet Joel; And it shall come to pass in the last days, saith God, I will pour out of my Spirit upon all flesh: and your sons and your daughters shall prophesy, and your young men shall see visions, and your old men shall dream dreams: And on my servants and on my handmaidens I will pour out in those days of my Spirit; and they shall prophesy: And I will shew wonders in heaven above, and signs in the earth beneath; blood, and fire, and vapour of smoke: The sun shall be turned into darkness, and the moon into blood, before that great and notable day of the Lord come: And it shall come to pass, that whosoever shall call on the name of the Lord shall be saved" (Acts 2:14-21).

As the astonished crowd heard the believers speaking in other tongues, "And they were all amazed, and were in doubt, saying one to another, What meaneth this? Others mocking said, These men are full of new wine" (Acts 2:12, 13). But Peter boldly proclaimed that ". . . this is that which was spoken by the prophet Joel" (Acts 2:16), and he went on to repeat Joel's prophecy which is recorded in Joel 2:28-32. In other words, Peter explained, this manifestation which the people were witnessing had been foretold by God's prophet centuries before, and it heralded a new dispensation, a new day of God's grace, and the beginning of the "last days" which Joel referred to. Today we are living in the end of these "last days."

One of the fulfillments of Joel's prophecy and the outpouring of the spirit was that ". . . your young men shall see visions." (Joel 2:28). The AMPLIFIED BIBLE says, "your young men shall see . . . divinely granted appearances" (Acts 2:17). In these next few pages I want to tell about one of these divinely granted appearances that I had when I was a young man of thirty-three years of age.

At the time of this experience I was conducting a tent revival in Rockwall, Texas, during the latter part of August and the first part of September, 1950. On Saturday, September 2, it rained all day—not a hard, driving rain, but a slow, gentle, soaking rain. It was still raining that evening at church time, and when we arrived at the tent there were only about forty people present. Rockwall is in the blackland of north-central Texas, and someone has said that if you stick with the blackland when it is dry, it will stick with you when it is wet. Many of the people who had been attending the meetings lived in the country, and they couldn't get to the service because of the rain and mud. For this reason the crowd was small that Saturday night.

As everyone present was a Christian, I just gave a Bible lesson and then invited the folks to come to the altar to pray. We gathered around the altar around nine-thirty. Let me say here that I no more expected what was to follow than I could have expected to be the first man ever to land on the moon. I hadn't been doing any unusual praying or fasting. I had not been praying that I would have such an experience. In fact, I hadn't even thought about such a thing.

Everyone was praying around the altar, and I knelt on the platform beside a folding chair near the pulpit. I began to pray in the spirit, that is, to pray in other tongues. While praying in other tongues I heard a voice say to me, "Come up hither." At first I didn't realize that the voice was really speaking to me. I thought everybody heard it.

"Come up hither," the voice said again. Then I looked and it seemed that Jesus was standing about where the top of the tent would be. As I looked up again, the tent had disappeared, the folding chairs had disappeared, every tent pole had disappeared, the pulpit had disappeared, and God permitted me to see into the spirit realm.

Jesus was standing there, and I stood in His presence. He was holding a soul-winner's crown. This crown was so extraordinarily beautiful that human language could not begin to describe it. Jesus said that the crown was for every one of His children, but they were often too busy. They put off His commands and say, "Lord, I will do that later," and souls are lost because they will not obey Him.

When Jesus said that, I wept before Him. I knelt down and repented of my failures. Then Jesus said to me again, "Come up hither." It seemed that I went with Him through the air until we came to a beautiful city. We did not actually go into the city but we beheld it at close range as one might go up on a mountain overlooking a city and look down on the city in the valley. Its beauty was beyond words!

Jesus said that people say they are ready for heaven. They talk about their mansions and about the glories of heaven while many all around them are in darkness and have no hope. He said I should share my hope with them and invite them to come with me.

Then Jesus turned to me and said, "Now let us go down to hell." We came back down out of heaven, and when we came to earth we didn't stop but kept going. Numerous Scriptures in the Bible refer to hell as being beneath us. For example, "Hell from beneath is moved for thee to meet thee at thy coming . . . thou shalt be brought down to hell" (Isaiah 14:9, 15). "Therefore hell hath enlarged herself . . . and he that rejoiceth, shall descend into it" (Isaiah 5:14).

We went down to hell, and as we went into that place I saw what appeared to be human beings wrapped in flames. I said, "Lord, this looks just as it did when I saw it on that Saturday night, April 22, 1933, when I died and came to this place. Then You spoke and I came back up out of here. I then repented and prayed, seeking Your forgiveness, and You saved me. Only now I feel so different. I am not afraid. Nor am I as horrified as I was then."

Jesus told me to warn men and women about this place, and I cried out with tears that I would.

He then brought me back to earth. I became aware that I was kneeling on the platform by the folding chair, and Jesus stood by my side. As He stood there He talked to me about my ministry. He told me some things in general that He later explained in more detail in another vision. Then Jesus disappeared and I realized that I was still kneeling on the platform. I could hear the people praying all around me.

About that time the Holy Spirit came upon me again. It seemed as if a wind was blowing on me, and I fell flat on my face on the platform. As I lay under the power of God, it seemed that I stood on a plain somewhere and could see for miles and miles around me, just as one can stand on one of the great plains of our nation and gaze off into the distance for miles in every direction.

I looked in every direction, but I couldn't see a sign of life anywhere. There were no trees or grass, no flowers or vegetation of any kind. There were no birds or animals. I felt so lonely. As I looked to the west I saw what appeared to be a tiny dot on the horizon. At first it was the only moving thing that I could see and so I continued to look at it. As I watched it I saw that it was growing larger and was coming toward me. I continued to watch it until it began to take on shape and form.

Soon I could see that it was a horse. As it came still closer I could see a man upon the horse, riding toward me at full speed. I watched him as he approached. He held the reins of the horse's bridle in his right hand, and he held a scroll of paper in his left hand high above his head.

As I said, I was not conscious of my earthly surroundings, but seemed to be standing high on a plain somewhere in space. When the horseman came to me, he pulled on the reins of the horse and stopped in front of me. I stood on his right; he passed the scroll from his left hand to his right hand, and handed it to me.

As I unrolled the scroll, which was a roll of paper twelve or fourteen inches long, he said, "Take and read." At the top of the page in big, bold, black print were the words, "WAR AND DESTRUCTION." I was struck dumb. He laid his right hand on my head and said, "Read, in the name of Jesus Christ." I began to read what followed on the paper, and as the words instructed me, I looked and saw what I read about.

First of all I read about thousands upon thousands of men in uniform. Then I looked and saw these men marching, wave after wave of soldiers marching as to war. I looked in the direction they were going, and as far as I could see there were thousands of men marching.

I turned to read the scroll again, and then looked and saw what I had just read about. I saw many women—some old with snowy white hair, some middle-aged, others were young women, and some were teen-agers. Some of the younger ones held babies in their arms. All of the women were bowed together in sorrow and were weeping profusely. Those who did not carry babies held their hands on their stomachs as they bowed over and wept. Tears flowed from their eyes like water.

I looked at the scroll again, and again I looked up to see what I had read about. I saw the skyline of a large city. Looking closer I saw its buildings were burned-out hulls, and portions of the city were in ruins. It was not written that just one city would be destroyed, burned, and in ruins, but that there would be many such cities.

The scroll was written in the first person and seemed as if Jesus Himself were speaking. I read, "America is receiving her last call. Some nations have already received their last call and will never receive another." Then in larger print it said, "The time of the end of all things is at hand." This statement was repeated four or five times.

It went on to say, "All the gifts of the spirit will be in operation in the church in these last days. The church will do greater things than even the early church did. It will have greater power, signs, and wonders than were recorded in the Acts of the Apostles. We have seen and experienced many healings, but we now behold amazing miracles such as have not been seen before.

More and more miracles will be performed in the last days which are just ahead (referring to the end of the last days), for it is time for the gift of the working of miracles to be more in prominence. We now have entered into the area of the miraculous. Many of my own people will not accept the moving of my Spirit, and will turn back and will not be ready to meet Me at my coming. Many will be deceived by false prophets and miracles of Satanic origin. But follow Me and you will not be deceived. I am gathering my own together and am preparing them, for the time is short."

There were several other exhortations to watchfulness, to awake and to pray and not to be deceived. Then I read, "As it was in the days of Noah, so also shall the coming of the Son of Man be. As I spoke to Noah and said, 'Yet seven days and I will cause it to rain upon the earth, forty days and forty nights, and every living substance will I destroy from off the face of the earth,' so today I am speaking and giving America her last warning and call to repentance, and the time that is left is comparable to the last seven days of Noah's time.

"Warn this generation, as did Noah his generation, for judgment is about to fall. And these sayings shall be fulfilled shortly, for I am coming soon. This is the last revival. I am preparing my people for my coming. Judgment is coming, but I will call my people away, even unto myself, before the worst shall come. But be thou faithful and watch and pray." Then the message concluded with the words, "For the time of the end of all things is at hand."

Those who were present that night under the tent at the time of this portion of the vision said that I read the scroll aloud for about thirty minutes. I handed the scroll back to the rider and he rode away in the direction from which he had come.

Then I was conscious of the fact that I still lay flat on my face on the floor, and for a few minutes I remained there, feeling the glory of this miraculous visitation. Again I heard a voice say, "Come up hither." And this time the voice said, "Come up hither, come up to the throne of God."

I saw Jesus standing again about where the top of the tent should be, and I went to Him through the air. When I reached Him, together we continued on to heaven. We came to the throne of God, and I beheld it in all its splendor. I was not able to look upon the face of God, but only beheld His form.

The first thing that attracted my attention was the rainbow about the throne. It was very beautiful. The second thing I noticed was the winged creatures on either side of the throne. They were peculiar looking creatures, and as I walked up with Jesus these creatures stood with wings outstretched. They were saying something, but they ceased and folded their wings. They had eyes of fire set all the way around their heads, and they looked in all directions at once.

I stood with Jesus in the midst, about eighteen to twenty-four feet from the throne. I looked at the rainbow first, at the winged creatures second, and then I started to look at the One who sat upon the throne. Jesus told me not to look upon His face. I could see only a form of a Being seated upon the throne.

Then for the first time I actually looked into the eyes of Jesus. Many times when relating this experience I am asked, "What did His eyes look like?" All I can say is that they looked like wells of living love. It seemed as if one could see a half mile deep into them, and the tender look of love is indescribable. As I looked into His face and into His eyes, I fell at His feet. I noticed then that His feet were bare, and I laid the palms of my hands on the top of His feet and laid my forehead on the backs of my hands. Weeping I said, "Oh, Lord, no one as unworthy as I should look upon Your face."

Jesus said that I should stand upright on my feet. I stood up.

He called me worthy to look upon His face, for He had called me and cleansed me from all sin. Then He went on to say that He had called me before I was born. Satan had tried to destroy my life before I was born and has tried many times since, but His angels have watched over me and have cared for me until this present hour. He told me that even as He appeared to my mother before I was born and told her to fear not, the child would be born, I would minister in the power of the spirit and would fulfill the ministry that He has called me to.

Then He talked to me about the last church I had pastored, in February, 1949, saying that at that time I had entered into the first phase of my ministry. Some ministers that He has actually called to the ministry live and die without getting into the first phase that He has for them. That is one reason that many ministers die prematurely—they are living only in His permissive will.

For those fifteen years I had been in only His permissive will. I had been a pastor for twelve years and had been in evangelistic work for three. During those years God had permitted me to do it, but it wasn't His perfect will for my life. And He said that I hadn't been waiting on Him, He had been waiting for me to obey Him.

Then He talked about that time when I entered into the first phase of my ministry in 1949, about how I had been unfaithful and hadn't done what He had told me to do, and that I didn't tell the people what He told me to tell them. I answered, "Lord, I wasn't unfaithful. I did obey You. I left my church and went out in the evangelistic field."

"Yes," He said, "you left the church and went out in evangelistic work. But you didn't do what I told you to do. The reason that you didn't is that you doubted it was my Spirit that had spoken to you. You see, faith obeys my Word whether it is the written Word of God or my Spirit that has spoken unto man."

I fell down before Him saying, "Yes, Lord, I have failed and I am sorry." I repented with many tears because I had missed His will and had doubted His dealings with me.

"Stand up on your feet," He said. As I stood before Him again, He told me that I had entered into the second phase of my ministry in January, 1950, and at that time He had spoken to me by prophecy and by the still small voice in my heart. In the eight months since then, during this second phase of my ministry, I had believed, I had been faithful, and I had obeyed. Now I was to enter into the third phase. If I would be faithful to what He told me, if I would believe and obey Him, then He would appear to me again. At that time I would enter into the fourth and final phase of my ministry.

Then the Lord said to me, "Stretch forth thine hand." He held His own hands out before Him and I looked into them. For some reason I expected to see a scar where the nail had pierced His flesh and had since grown together. I should have known better, but many times we get ideas that are not really Scriptural, yet they are accepted beliefs. I saw in the palms of His hands the wounds of the crucifixion—three-cornered, jagged holes. Each hole was large enough so that I could put my finger in it. I could see light on the other side of the hole.

After the vision, I got out my Bible and turned to the twentieth chapter of John's gospel to read about when Christ appeared to His disciples following His resurrection. When He first appeared to them, Thomas was not with them. They told Thomas that they had seen the Lord, but Thomas was unbelieving and said, ". . . Except I shall see in his hands the print of the nails, and put my finger into the print of the nails, and thrust my hand into his side, I will not believe" (John 20:25). Eight days later while the disciples, including Thomas, were together in a room, Jesus appeared in their midst. He turned to Thomas and said, ". . . Reach hither thy finger, and behold my hands; and reach hither thy hand, and thrust it into my side: and be not faithless, but believing." Then Thomas, knowing it was Jesus, exclaimed, ". . . My Lord and my God" (John 20:27, 28).

I had a deeper insight then into what Thomas had seen. He could have put his finger into the wound in Jesus' hand, as well as thrusting his hand into the Lord's side.

And so as I looked upon the wounds in His hands outstretched before me, I did as He instructed and held my hands out in front of me. He placed the finger of His right hand in the palm of my right hand and then my left. The moment He did, my hands began to burn as if a coal of fire had been placed in them.

Then Jesus told me to kneel down before Him. When I did so He laid His hand upon my head, saying that He had called me and given me a special anointing to minister to the sick. He went on to instruct me that when I would pray and lay hands upon the sick I was to lay one hand on each side of the body. If I felt the fire jump from hand to hand, an evil spirit or demon was present in the body causing the affliction. I should call him out in His name and the demon or demons would have to go. If the fire, or anointing, in my hand does not jump from hand to hand, it is a case of healing only. I should pray for the person in His name, and if he will believe and accept it, the anointing will leave my hands and go into his body, driving out the disease and bringing healing. When the fire, or the anointing, leaves my hands and goes into his body, I will know he is healed.

I fell at His feet and pleaded, "Lord, don't send me. Send somebody else, Lord, please don't send me. Just give me a little church to pastor somewhere. I would rather not go, Lord. I have heard so much criticism of those who pray for the sick. I just want a commonplace ministry."

Jesus rebuked me saying that He would go with me and stand by my side as I prayed for the sick. Sometimes I would see Him, and occasionally He would open the eyes of someone in the audience who will see Him and say, "I saw Jesus standing by that man while he was ministering to the sick."

He went on to ask who had called me, Him or the people?

"Well, You did, Lord."

He explained that I should fear Him and not people, because people may criticize me, but they are not my judge. I will stand before His judgment seat one day and will give an account unto Him for what I have done with this ministry, whether I have used it rightly or wrongly.

"All right, Lord," I said. "If You will go with me I will go and will do my best. I will be as faithful as I know how to be." Then there swelled up within my heart a love such as I have never known for those who criticize this type of ministry, and I said, "Lord, I will pray for them, for they don't know or they would not say the things they do. I myself have said similar things, never realizing as of course they do not. Forgive them, Lord."

"Go thy way, Son. Fulfill thy ministry and be thou faithful, for the time is short."

As I walked away from the throne of God, Jesus told me to give all the praise, honor and glory to Him for all that is done in His name; also, to be careful about money. Many of His servants whom He has anointed for this type of ministry have become money-minded and have lost the anointing and ministry that He gave them. There are many who would pay a great deal to be well. There are parents with children whose bodies are crippled and twisted. They would give thousands of dollars for their children's healing. Many of these shall be delivered as hands are laid upon them. But I must not accept a charge for my ministry, only offerings as I have been doing. I must be faithful for the time is short, He advised.

I thank God that I have seen polio-stricken children delivered and made well and straight, some of them walking, others in time becoming well.

-out cities

...ots we have had in ou...

...ortions of them were burned a...

...nd judgment is yet to come. The only

...save America from the judgment of God is genuine

...entance—a turning to God.

In the vision, Jesus said that all the gifts of the spirit would be in operation in the church in these last days. He said that the church would do greater things than the early church had done, which are recorded in the Acts of the Apostles. And I have seen this fulfilled in the years since then. In my own ministry I have seen miraculous healings as marvelous as any we read about in the Bible.

The third chapter of Acts tells of the man who was lame from birth who sat daily at the gate of the temple begging alms of those who entered. Peter said, ". . . Silver and gold have I none; but such as I have give I thee: In the name of Jesus Christ of Nazareth rise up and walk" (Acts 3:6). The man was instantly healed. He leaped and walked, he praised God for his deliverance. We see in our ministry today cripples who are healed in the name of Jesus.

On the Day of Pentecost one hundred and twenty people were

of others,
awaiting His coming,
und the world just as many grea
in the Acts of the Apostles.

In the vision, when Jesus was telling me about
anointing that He was giving me He said, "If the anointing le
you, fast and pray until it comes back." Now whenever the
anointing wanes, I wait upon the Lord in prayer and fasting, and
the same anointing comes upon me again.

I no longer lay one hand on each side of the person I am praying for to see if an evil spirit is causing the affliction because the
Lord gave me a vision two years later, which I will tell about in
more detail in another chapter.

In this first vision, the Lord told me that He would appear to
me again, and He has on several occasions. In the vision two
years later He said, "From this moment on, the gift that is known
in my Word as the gift of discerning of spirits will operate in
your ministry." With the operation of this gift, I can know when
a person's body is oppressed by an evil spirit, and, therefore, I
use this greater ministry.

Regarding the fact that Jesus said in the vision, "I called you
before you were born and separated you from your mother's

womb," this was contrary to my belief at that time. However, looking further into God's Word I read where the Lord said the same thing to Jeremiah concerning his ministry—that the Lord called him before he was born.

A week after this vision appeared to me, my mother was visiting me and I related it to her. I told her how the Lord said to me, "I called you before you were born. I separated you from your mother's womb. Satan tried to destroy your life before you were born and has tried many times since, but my angels have watched over you and have cared for you until thi⬛⬛⬛⬛⬛ Even as I appeared to your mother bef⬛⬛⬛⬛⬛ told her to fear not, the child would be ⬛⬛⬛⬛ ness concerning my second coming."

When Mother heard this she almost jumped ⬛⬛⬛ During the months before I was born she was having ma⬛⬛ culties. My father was away much of the time, and she di⬛⬛ know where he was. She didn't have adequate food to eat. He⬛ parents lived less than three blocks away, but as they had opposed her marrying my father, she was reluctant to go back home and ask them for help. "I was just too proud to ask them for anything," she told me.

"Not having enough food, I became ill, and for the baby's sake I decided to swallow my pride and go to my parents and ask for something to eat. This was just a few days before you were born prematurely. I started down the street and when I got as far as just in front of Aunt Mary's house, I heard a sound like wind blowing through the trees. I could hear tree leaves stirring. Yet, there was not one single tree anywhere near. I became frightened, and I looked up to the sky. It was a bright, sunny August day. Not a cloud dotted the pure blue sky.

"I walked on a few steps, and heard the sound again like wind blowing through a tree. I looked up again and this time I saw one white cloud. It seemed at first to be just hanging in the sky.

Then it began to descend, and as it did a form took shape upon it. It came right down out of the sky and stood before me. Jesus said, 'Fear not, the child shall be born, for he shall bear witness concerning my second coming.' He was trying to tell me that my child would take part in the revival that would usher in the coming of the Son of Man. He would not be the only one, of course, but would have a part in the great last move of God's Spirit. But I became so frightened that I began to run, and I ran the rest of the way to my mother's house.

"When ████████ arrived there, pale and out of breath, my mother ███████ 'You look like you've just seen a ghost!' I im- ███████ I had just witnessed, but I never did tell ███████ never would talk about it either, as we just ███████ such things and were afraid that people would ███████ lost my mind."

███████ I listened to my mother tell of her experience before I was born, it fit right in with what the Lord had shown me in this vision.

3

If–The Badge of Doubt

My next vision of Jesus appeared to me about a month after the first vision. I was conducting a revival meeting in the state of Oklahoma. I had told the congregation what the Lord had shown me about ministering to the sick, and the anointing with God's healing power in my hands. One night while we were ministering to the sick, a man came before me in the healing line who told me he had tuberculosis of the spine. He had been through three different clinics and all of the doctors had given the same diagnosis. They had said he was beyond medical aid at this time. The man's spine was as stiff as a board.

In praying for him I laid one hand on his chest and one hand on his back. When I did, the fire, or the anointing, jumped from hand to hand. I knew immediately that his body was oppressed by an evil spirit. I commanded the spirit saying, "You foul spirit that oppresses this man's body, I command you to come out of his body in the name of the Lord Jesus Christ." And then I made a terrible mistake. I got into unbelief. It is easy to get into unbelief sometimes, no matter who we are, and not even realize it.

I said to the man, "See *if* you can stoop over and bend your back. Try to touch your toes." The word "if" is the badge of doubt. When I said, "See *if* you can,"—that was doubt. God will put up with a certain amount of doubt in a young Christian who doesn't know any better, but when one is enlightened in God's Word, the Lord won't let him get by with it.

The man tried to bend over, of course, but he couldn't. His back was as stiff as it ever had been. Then I laid my hands upon him again, one hand on his chest and one hand on his back, and I felt the fire jump from hand to hand. Again I commanded, "You foul spirit that oppresses this man's body, I command you to come out of him in the name of the Lord Jesus Christ." Then the second time I said to the man, "See *if* you can stoop over. Bend your back and touch your toes."

Of course, his back was as immovable as before because I was acting in unbelief and didn't realize it.

Then I said, "Well, we will *try* (which too is unbelief) the third time," and I laid one hand on his chest and the other on his back. Again, I had the manifestation of the anointing in my hands. For the third time, I said, "You foul spirit that oppresses this man's body, I command you to come out of him in the name of the Lord Jesus Christ." To the man I said, "Now see *if* you can stoop over. See *if* you can bend down." He couldn't, of course. He tried, but he couldn't bend his back.

I gave up and went on to pray for the next person. The man walked back down the aisle.

I was standing on the platform, about three feet to the right of the pulpit. Just as the next person stepped up to be prayed for, for some unknown reason I looked over to my left. I saw Jesus standing there as plainly as any man I had ever seen in my life. I thought everybody saw Him, but I learned later that no one in the congregation saw Him or heard Him speak, except me. The congregation heard what I said, but they didn't see or hear anyone else.

Jesus was standing beside the pulpit. I could have reached out my hand to touch Him. As He stood there, He pointed His finger at me and said, "I said that in my name the demon or demons will leave."

"Lord, I know You said that. It has been only a month since You appeared to me in Rockwall, Texas, and told me to command the demon or demons to come out in Your name. I told the demon to come out of that man, but he didn't come out."

Again, Jesus pointed His finger at me and said, "*I* said, in my name to call out the demons and they *will leave* the body."

"I know You said that, Lord, and I commanded the spirit to leave this man's body in the name of the Lord Jesus Christ, but he didn't go."

Then the third time, Jesus put His finger in my face and said, "*I said in my name the demons will go!* Call them out in my name and they will leave the body in my name."

Weakly, I replied again, "Lord, I know You said that. It happened just a month ago and it is as fresh on my mind as though You said it last night. I know what You told me. And I did tell that demon to leave this man's body, but he didn't go."

Then I think I knew how Jesus must have looked when He drove the money-changers out of the temple, as recorded in the eleventh chapter of Mark's gospel. Suddenly it seemed as if His eyes shot fire; I could see flashes of lightning in them. For the fourth time He jabbed His finger at me and said emphatically, "*Yes, but I said the demons will go!*" Then He disappeared.

I realized then that I had acted in unbelief. We sometimes get to thinking that if we have a special gift or anointing to minister, it will always work. But that is not the case. No matter how much authority we might have, no matter how many special gifts we may have or how much power we might possess, it works by faith and by faith only.

When I realized that I had exercised doubt instead of faith, I saw my mistake. I called the man to come back to the platform.

He was standing at the rear of the auditorium and hadn't gone back to his seat as yet. I do not know how long this vision lasted, whether he had not had time to return to his seat yet or whether he had stopped because he heard me talking and was listening to what I was saying. At any rate, he was still standing at the back.

I pointed to him and said, "Come back up here, brother." He retraced his steps back up the aisle. I stood on the platform waiting for him to come around the altar to where I was. The instant he stood before me I slapped him on the back and with my other hand on his chest I said, "Satan, I told you to leave this body. Out you go in the name of the Lord Jesus Christ!" Then I said to the man, "Now, my brother (I didn't put an *if* in it this time), stoop over and touch your toes."

Instantly, his back was limber. The tuberculosis of the spine was gone. The spine which had been as stiff as a board was healed. He could stoop over and touch his toes as well as any normal person can. He was completely well!

As this man had come over to our meeting from Arkansas, we didn't see him any more until two weeks later. He came back to be in the service on the last Sunday night of the meeting. I asked him if he was still able to stoop over and touch his toes. "Yes, I am still free," he said with a big smile lighting his face. He stepped out into the aisle, stooped over, touched the floor, and went through several exercises to prove that he was still limber and free.

This experience demonstrated to me once and for all the importance of following God's Word explicitly. And I learned that no matter who we are, if we move in unbelief, we will stop the flow of God's power.

4

How Satan Influences Lives Today

My third vision of Jesus occurred in December, 1952, in Broken Bow, Oklahoma, where I was conducting a meeting in a Full Gospel church. I was staying in the parsonage with the pastor and his wife and eleven-year-old daughter during my two-week stay there. One night after the service, we had retired to the parsonage and were having a sandwich and a glass of milk in the kitchen. As we ate, we discussed some of the things we had gone over in the Bible lesson we had given that evening. As we talked about the things of the Lord, time slipped away from us.

His little girl was sitting there with us, and finally she became sleepy and said, "Daddy, it's getting late, and I have to get up early in the morning to go to school. Won't you come pray with me now?" It was their custom that he always pray with her at night and then tuck her into bed.

He looked at his watch and said, "It's eleven-thirty! Why, I never dreamed it was that late. We have been sitting here talking for two hours." Then he said to his daughter, "Come here, honey, and we'll just kneel down here and Brother Hagin can have prayer with us. Then you can go to bed."

As we knelt together in that kitchen, each of us beside a chair,

I was in the spirit before my knees ever touched the floor. To some who might wonder what it means to be "in the spirit," let me refer to what the Bible says about it. When the Apostle John was on the isle of Patmos, the Bible says he ". . . was in the Spirit on the Lord's day, and heard behind me a great voice, as of a trumpet, Saying, I am Alpha and Omega, the first and the last: and, What thou seest, write in a book . . ." (Revelation 1:10, 11). The Lord Himself appeared unto John, speaking with him and telling him of things to come. He gave him a message to give to the six churches in Asia Minor, and all that we have in the Book of Revelation.

The Bible also tells of the time when Peter was "in the spirit." In the tenth chapter of Acts we read where Peter fell into a trance and saw a vision. In the vision he saw a great sheet that was let down from heaven from its four corners, and all kinds of animals, birds, and creeping things, beasts both clean and unclean were on this sheet. Peter heard a voice saying, ". . . Rise, Peter; kill, and eat. But Peter said, Not so, Lord; for I have never eaten any thing that is common or unclean" (Acts 10:13, 14). In this vision, the Lord told Peter to take the gospel of salvation to the Gentiles. Up until this time the gospel had been limited to the Jews.

We notice the words in the tenth verse of this passage in Acts that Peter "fell into a trance." When this happens, the physical senses are suspended. This doesn't mean that the person is unconscious or that he has fainted. It simply means that the physical senses are not operating at the moment that the person is caught up into the spirit. God permits him to see into the spirit realm, or to see whatever He wants him to see.

On this December night in 1952 in the kitchen of the parsonage, my physical senses were suspended. At that moment I wouldn't have known that I was kneeling beside a kitchen chair.

It just seemed as if I knelt down into a white cloud that enveloped me.

Immediately I saw Jesus. He seemed to be standing above me, about as high as the ceiling is from the floor. He began to talk to me. "I am going to teach you concerning demons and evil spirits," He began, "for from this night forward, what is known in my Word as the gift of discerning of spirits will operate in your ministry when you are in the spirit."

Before I go any further in relating this vision, let me explain something which I feel is very significant. Notice that Jesus said, "When you are in the spirit, this will operate." Many times we seem to think that man operates these gifts of the spirit. However, man doesn't do it. They are manifested through him by the Holy Spirit. "But the manifestation of the Spirit is given to every man to profit withal" (1 Corinthians 12:7). We do not have a thing in the world to do with it other than the fact that it is manifested *through* us.

Jesus said to me, "When you are in the spirit, this will operate." It won't operate just at any given time we might want it to operate. In other words, we cannot push a button and turn it on and off.

To illustrate, let me tell of just two incidents that have happened in my ministry. The first happened the very next month following this vision. I was conducting a meeting in the Rose Center Assembly of God Church in Tyler, Texas, in January, 1953. Reverend D. D. Lewis was the pastor. I had been invited to stay with the Lewises during the meeting, and I arrived at the parsonage on Saturday before the meeting was to start on Sunday.

After helping me with my luggage and showing me to my room, Brother Lewis sat down to talk with me while I unpacked my suitcases. In the course of our conversation he said, "I trust that my niece will receive her healing while you are here." Then he went on to explain that she had cancer of the lungs. As his brother was not financially able to pay the girl's medical bills, Brother Lewis had taken on the responsibility. "I put her through one clinic and wasn't satisfied with their diagnosis," he said, "so I put her through another clinic. Both of them confirmed that as far as they could determine from all the tests they could run without performing surgery, she had cancer of the left lung.

"The doctors insisted on operating immediately, saying, 'Even if we take out one lung, she could live. But she cannot live without any lung.' When my niece said she would like to wait a week before undergoing surgery so she could fast and pray about it, the doctors said, 'Then it may be too late, for in a week's time it may spread too far.'

"Nevertheless, she insisted on a week's time to fast and pray. At the end of the week she decided not to have the operation. She said, 'I knew two women both of whom had cancer of the lung. One was operated on, the other wasn't—both of them died. One just lived a couple of years longer. What is two years? I will trust God to heal me and if He doesn't, if I die, I'll die.'

"Many weeks have now come and gone and she is bedfast. The doctors say it is too late for an operation as the cancer has spread to both lungs. They are feeding her six times a day, but she is still losing weight. We are planning to bring her to your services for prayer."

It was my custom at that time, when ministering in smaller churches such as this, to have special healing services on Tuesday and Friday nights of each week. On the first Tuesday night, they got the girl out of bed and brought her to the service. I ministered to her by the laying on of hands, but nothing happened. On Friday night the same thing happened. The same thing happened on Tuesday night, and again on Friday night of the following week. Four times I had laid hands on her and nothing happened. I say this to point out that if it were just me exercising the gifts of the spirit, I would already have done it. But remember that Jesus said, "When you are *in the spirit,* this discerning of spirits will operate."

We continued the meeting on into the third week, and on Tuesday of the third week they brought her to church again. When she stood before me this time I was suddenly in the spirit. Suddenly the Spirit of God enveloped me like a cloud.

Such an experience is similar to the Old Testament account of the dedication of Solomon's Temple. When the singers and musicians all became as one in praising God, and the people lifted their voices to praise God, the glory of the Lord, or the cloud of the Lord, filled the temple so that the priest couldn't stand to minister (1 Kings 8:10, 11). It was this same sort of cloud that descended on me. I was in the spirit, the glory of God, the cloud of God. My eyes were wide open, but every person in the church disappeared. Every pew disappeared, the altar disappeared, the pulpit disappeared.

This young girl and I were standing in the midst of the white cloud. As I looked at her I saw fastened to the outside of her body, over her left lung (for this is where the cancer started), an evil spirit, or an imp. He looked very similar to a small monkey hanging onto her body, as a monkey would hang onto a tree limb.

God permitted me to see into the realm of the spirit to see this evil spirit. I addressed him and said, "You foul spirit that oppresses this girl's body, you will have to leave." No one else in the congregation saw or heard anything but me. But they did hear what I said.

Then the evil spirit spoke and said, "I know I will have to leave if you tell me to, but I don't want to."

"In the name of the Lord Jesus Christ, I command you to leave this body," I said. I watched as the evil spirit turned loose of the girl and fell to the floor. Then I said, "Not only must you leave this body, but you must also leave this building." He ran down the aisle of the church and out the door.

Immediately the girl lifted her hands and began praising God saying, "I am free, I am free." Although she had been a member of a Full Gospel church for fifteen years—since she was a child of eight—she had been seeking the baptism of the Holy Spirit, but had not received. In this instant, she received the Holy Spirit and began to speak with other tongues as the Spirit of God gave her utterance.

That same week she went back to her doctors and requested new X rays and tests of her lungs. She still looked no better outwardly.

She was frail and run-down. The doctors told her that more tests were not necessary. They had done everything they could do for her. She insisted, however, and so they began to make new X rays and to run the usual tests. "Something has happened!" the doctors exclaimed, and they ran another set of tests and took more X rays. Finally convinced, they said, "We cannot find any trace of cancer. It is all gone. Your lungs are clear. We wouldn't have believed it possible if we didn't have the X rays and tests ourselves to prove that you had cancer. What happened to you?"

She explained exactly what had happened, that it was God's power that had made her completely whole. They said, "Well, all we can say is that we know the condition you were in and that you are now completely well. And if you like, we will sign an affidavit stating that you had cancer of the lungs, but that now it is gone."

The point I am making is that if it had been me operating this gift, I would have done so the first time I prayed for her rather than the fifth time. This is what Jesus meant when He said, "This will operate when you are in the spirit."

A similar incident took place several years later in 1958 when I was conducting a meeting in Pueblo, Colorado. While we were having special prayer for the sick one night, a man from Colorado Springs came forward for prayer. He told me that he was nervous, couldn't sleep, and that he was on tranquilizers. His wife later told me that they were about to commit him to a mental institution.

I laid hands on him and prayed for his healing, that his nerves would be healed and that his body would be healed from the top of his head to the soles of his feet. Then I went on to pray for the next person in the healing line. I continued praying for other folks for about ten minutes more. This man had gone back to his seat, which was on my right. When I looked over at him, immediately I was in the spirit. God permitted me to see into the realm of the spirit, and I saw an evil spirit sitting on this man's shoulder. The spirit's arms were around the man's head in an armlock. I could see this but no one else in the congregation was aware of what was going on.

I called the man to come to me, and when he stood in front of me I said, "You foul spirit that oppresses this man's mind, I command you to leave his body right now in the name of Jesus." When I said that, the spirit turned loose of him and fell to the floor.

The evil spirit said to me, "I didn't want to leave this man, but I know that if you tell me to I have to."

"Not only are you to leave this body, but you are to leave this building at once!" I commanded, and he ran out the side door.

A broad smile crossed the man's face. He threw his hands into the air and shouted, "I am free! I am free!" Although I hadn't mentioned what I had seen in the vision, the man said, "It seemed as if an iron band was around my head, being screwed tighter and tighter. More and more pressure was being put on it. Suddenly it just popped off and was gone."

Do such healings last? Ten years later we heard from this man when he called our office in Tulsa for prayer for one of his children. He was still rejoicing in his freedom from demon oppression.

These are just two of many examples I could give to illustrate the operation of the spirit in my life, and how it is not something which we can control but which operates as God wills. There are no magic buttons we can push to operate these things, but it is only as the Lord leads.

Many suppose that the apostles carried around these various spiritual gifts and operated them at will. But this certainly was not the case when Paul and Silas were at Philippi. They were there because God had led them into Macedonia by a vision. Lydia, a seller of purple dye, was saved as a result of their ministry.

Paul and Silas were in the city of Philippi for several days and while there, ". . . It came to pass, as we went to prayer, a certain damsel possessed with a spirit of divination met us, which brought her masters much gain by soothsaying: The same followed Paul and us, and cried, saying, These men are the servants of the most high God, which shew unto us the way of salvation" (Acts 16:16, 17).

This girl had a spirit of divination, which is soothsaying or fortune-telling. She knew who Paul and Silas were by the spirit that was in her. In other words, that spirit knew them. She didn't know them for she had never seen them before. Yet she said, "These men are the servants of the most high God. . . ."

Then we read, "And this did she many days. But Paul, being grieved, turned and said to the spirit, I command thee in the name of Jesus Christ to come out of her. And he came out the same hour" (Acts 16:18).

It is evident that Paul had the gift of discerning of spirits in operation in his ministry. Yet the Scripture says that the girl followed them around for many days. Why didn't Paul command the evil spirit to leave her on the first day? Why didn't he do it on the second day? The answer is simply that the gift didn't operate when Paul wanted it to operate, but as the spirit wills.

Until he had the operation of the spirit, he was just as helpless as any other person to deal with the situation.

We need to understand the Scriptures concerning this more fully in order to be open to God, and look to Him in prayer for the manifestation of His Spirit, the manifestation of the gifts of the spirit.

Getting back to the vision that God gave me late that night in Broken Bow, Oklahoma, the Lord said to me, "From this night forward, what is known as the gift of discerning of spirits will operate in your life when you are in the spirit. I will show you how these spirits get hold of people and dominate them, even Christians, if they allow them to do it."

He went on to say, "There are four classes of demons or evil spirits." He said that they are divided into four groups as mentioned in Ephesians. "For we wrestle not against flesh and blood, but against principalities, against powers, against the rulers of the darkness of this world, against spiritual wickedness [wicked spirits] in high places" (Ephesians 6:12).

The Lord said, "There are four divisions: principalities, powers, rulers of the darkness of this world, and wicked spirits in high places or in the heavenlies. The highest spirits with which you have to deal are the rulers of the darkness of this world."

He went on talking to me about the fact that the Word of God says that the whole world lieth in darkness, that we who are believers are children of light and not of darkness. He referred to a number of different Scriptures, only a few of which I will enumerate here.

"Be ye not unequally yoked together with unbelievers: for what fellowship hath righteousness with unrighteousness? and what communion hath light with darkness" (2 Corinthians 6:14)? Believers are called righteousness and unbelievers are called unrighteousness. The believer is called the light, and the unbeliever is called darkness.

The second chapter of Colossians tells of Christ's death on the cross and resurrection from the dead, "And having spoiled principalities and powers, he made a shew of them openly, triumphing over them in it" (verse 15). In other words, Christ, in His death, burial, and resurrection, spoiled or defeated these same principalities and powers that we must deal with.

In Colossians we read, "Giving thanks unto the Father, which hath made us meet to be partakers of the inheritance of the saints in light [notice the word "light"]: Who hath delivered us from the power of darkness [or authority of darkness], and hath translated us into the kingdom of his dear Son: In whom we have redemption through his blood, even the forgiveness of sins" (Colossians 1:12-14). We as the children of God are the children of light, and every child of the devil is a child of darkness. We are not in the kingdom of darkness; we are in God's Kingdom—the kingdom of light.

The Lord went on to say to me, "These are the highest types of demons with which you have to deal on earth—the rulers of the darkness of this world. They rule all unsaved people, all who are in darkness. They rule over them and dominate them. That is why people do and say things that they don't intend to. That is why some good people say, 'I would never do anything like that,' and before a year has passed they have done something worse. This is because they are dominated by the rulers of the darkness of this world. They are in the kingdom of darkness. And whether you want to admit it or not, even your close friends and relatives, or whoever it may be, if they are unsaved, are dominated by these spirits who are rulers of the darkness of this world.

"It is always one of these rulers of the darkness of this world that possesses a person. They rule not only those who are within the darkness of this world, but they also tell the principalities what to do. Then the principalities rule over the powers and tell them what to do. The lowest type of demons have very little to do. They do very little thinking of their own and are told what to do.

"Now I will show you how these evil spirits get hold of people when they are allowed to," the Lord said to me, and then suddenly in the vision I saw a woman. I immediately recognized her as being the former wife of a minister. I had been introduced to her and her husband on one occasion and shook hands with them. Other than that, I didn't know either of them and I had had no communication with either of them in any way. I only knew that she had since left her husband.

"This woman was a child of mine," the Lord said. "She was in the ministry with her husband. She was filled with the spirit, and even the gifts of the spirit were operating in her life. One day an evil spirit came to her and whispered in her ear, 'You are a beautiful woman. You could have had fame, popularity, and wealth, but you have been cheated in life by following in the Christian walk.' The woman realized that this was an evil spirit and she said, 'Get thee behind me, Satan.' The spirit left her for a period.

"By and by the same spirit returned. He sat on her shoulder and whispered in her ear, 'You are a beautiful woman, but you have been robbed by taking this lowly walk of Christianity and living this separated life.' Again she recognized this as Satan and said, 'Satan, I resist you in the name of Jesus,' and he left her for awhile.

"But he came back again and sat on her shoulder, whispering the same things in her ear. This time she began to entertain these thoughts, for she liked to think that she was beautiful. As she began to think along the lines that the devil suggested to her, she became obsessed with that thinking."

Then in the vision I saw the woman become as transparent as glass, and I saw in her mind a black dot. "That dot represents the fact that she is obsessed in her thinking with this spirit," the Lord said. "At first she was oppressed on the outside, but as she allowed the devil's suggestions to take hold of her thoughts, her mind became obsessed. She wanted to think, 'I am a beautiful woman. I could have wealth and popularity, but I have been robbed in life.' Still, it wasn't too late. She could have resisted; she could have refused to think those thoughts. Then the spirit would have fled from her and she would have remained free. But she chose otherwise.

"Finally she left her husband and went out into the world, seeking the fame and wealth which the devil offered. She took up with one man after another. After a time that thing got down into her spirit." In the vision I saw the black dot move from her head to her heart, and then the woman said, "I don't want the Lord any more. Just leave me alone."

I said, "Lord, why are You showing this to me? Do You want me to pray for this woman? Do You want me to cast the devil out of her?"

"No, I don't want you to pray and cast the devil out of her," the Lord answered, "because you couldn't anyway. She wants that spirit and as long as she wants it, she can have it."

"Then, why did You show this to me, Lord?"

"I have shown this to you for two reasons; first, so that you could see how an evil spirit will get hold of a person, even a child of God, if they will let him. Secondly, I want you to deal with that spirit who is operating through that woman and is harassing and intimidating the ministry of her former husband."

"How do I do that?" I asked. The minister was in the same state that I was in, but the woman was in another state.

"There is no distance in the realm of the spirit," the Lord said. "Simply speak to that spirit and command him, in my name, saying 'You foul spirit that is operating in the life of this woman [calling her name], that is harassing and embarrassing the ministry of the servant of the Lord [calling his name], I command you to desist in your operation and stop in your maneuvers this moment.'"

In the spirit, I said those words and immediately that spirit ceased to operate through her to intimidate that minister. From that day forward that minister was never troubled again by her or that spirit.

"Lord, what will happen to her?" I asked.

"She will spend eternity in the regions of the damned, where there is weeping and gnashing of teeth," He answered. And in the vision I saw her go down into the pit. I heard her awful screams.

"This woman was Your child, Lord. She was filled with Your Spirit and had part in the ministry. Yet You said not to pray for her. I cannot understand this."

The Lord reminded me of the following Scripture: "If any man see his brother sin a sin which is not unto death, he shall ask, and he shall give him life for them that sin not unto death. There is a sin unto death: I do not say that he shall pray for it" (1 John 5:16).

I said, "But, Lord, as a Baptist I have always believed that the sin referred to in this Scripture is physical death, and that the person is saved although he has sinned."

"But that Scripture doesn't say physical death," the Lord pointed out. "You are adding something to it. If you will read the entire fifth chapter of 1 John you will see that it is talking about life and death—spiritual life, and spiritual death, but this is spiritual death. This refers to a believer who can sin a sin unto death, and therefore I say that you shall not pray for it. For this reason I told you not to pray for this woman because she sinned a sin unto death."

"This really disrupts my theology, Lord. Would You explain

some more?" I asked. Sometimes we need our theology disrupted
if it is not in line with the Word.

Jesus reminded me of the following Scripture: "For it is impossible for those who were once enlightened, and have tasted
of the heavenly gift, and were made partakers of the Holy Ghost,
And have tasted the good word of God, and the powers of the
world to come, If they shall fall away, to renew them again unto
repentance; seeing they crucify to themselves the Son of God
afresh, and put him to an open shame" (Hebrews 6:4-6).

"Yes, I know that Scripture, but we Baptists have said that
this does not refer to the Christian—that it is just a lost person
getting under conviction."

Then the Lord said to me, "Remember that I told you that this
woman was my child, that she was filled with the Holy Ghost
and had part in the ministry. You will notice that the Scripture
says, 'It is impossible for those who were once enlightened [a
person enlightened by my Spirit concerning his lost condition is
what you call being under conviction] and have tasted of the
heavenly gift' (Hebrews 6:4). I am the heavenly gift. A man
under conviction is enlightened, but he has not tasted of Me, of
the heavenly gift. The Word of God says, 'For God so loved the
world, that he gave his only begotten Son, that whosoever believeth in him should not perish, but have everlasting life' (John
3:16). I am the heavenly gift, and the man under conviction
has not tasted of the heavenly gift. He sees his lost condition
and sees that he can be saved. 'For the wages of sin is death;
but the gift of God is eternal life through Jesus Christ our Lord'
(Romans 6:23). No one has tasted of the heavenly gift, the gift
of God, until he has received eternal life by accepting Me as
Lord and Saviour.

"Notice the words in this Scripture, '. . . and were made partakers of the Holy Ghost [this woman had been baptized in the
Holy Ghost], and have tasted the good word of God' (Hebrews

6:4, 5), or as the Phillips translation reads, '. . . who have known the wholesome nourishment of the Word of God. . . .' In other words, the meat of God's Word and not just the milk. Baby Christians cannot commit this sin. It is to be regretted that baby Christians live as they sometimes do, that they say and do some things they should not. But I do not hold these things against them any more than you would hold things a little child may do against him because he doesn't know any better. But the person referred to in this Scripture, and that includes the woman I am showing you, has tasted the good Word of God—that is, has grown beyond the baby Christian stage. One Scripture says, 'As newborn babes, desire the sincere milk of the word, that ye may grow thereby' (1 Peter 2:2). This woman had grown beyond the sincere milk of the Word. She had tasted the solid meat of the Word. She had already tasted of the 'powers of the world to come.' She had the gifts of the spirit in operation in her life.

"For one to commit 'a sin unto death,' he would have had all five of these experiences.

1. Be enlightened (or convicted) to see his lost state, to know that there is no way for him to be saved except through Jesus Christ.
2. Taste of the heavenly gift which is Jesus.
3. Become partaker of the Holy Ghost, or be filled with the Holy Ghost.
4. Grow enough out of the babyhood stage to have tasted the good Word of God.
5. Have the powers of the world-to-come operating in his life, or the gifts of the spirit.

"This woman had all these qualifications. And my Word says it is impossible, '. . . If they shall fall away, to renew them again unto repentance; seeing they crucify to themselves the Son of God afresh, and put him to an open shame'" (Hebrews 6:4-6).

I asked the Lord, "What sin is this then?"

The Lord referred me to the following Scripture: "For if we sin wilfully after that we have received the knowledge of the truth, there remaineth no more sacrifice for sins, But a certain fearful looking for of judgment and fiery indignation, which shall devour the adversaries. He that despised Moses' law died without mercy under two or three witnesses: Of how much sorer punishment, suppose ye, shall he be thought worthy, who hath trodden underfoot the Son of God, and hath counted the blood of the covenant, wherewith he was sanctified, an unholy thing, and hath done despite unto the Spirit of grace" (Hebrews 10:26-29)?

The Lord said to me, "The sin that this Scripture speaks about is that of the believer who turns his back upon Me. Notice the words in the Scripture, 'He that despised Moses' law died without mercy . . . Of how much sorer punishment, suppose ye, shall he be thought worthy, who hath trodden under foot the Son of God. . . .'

"Because of great persecution, the Hebrew Christians referred to in this passage of Scripture were tempted to go back to Judaism, but if they went back they would have trodden underfoot the Son of God. They would have counted the blood of the covenant an unholy thing, for they were saying that Jesus is not the Messiah, that He is not the Son of God. They turned their backs on Me. This is why Paul warned them that if they did that, it would be impossible to renew them unto repentance.

"It is sad that this woman left her husband for another man. But adultery is not the unpardonable sin. If she had turned back to Me in repentance, even though she might have had a hundred men, I would have forgiven her. Whatever she might have done, if she had asked Me to forgive her, I would have. Or even if

she had been a baby Christian when she said, 'I don't want
Jesus any more, leave me alone,' and didn't actually realize what
she was doing, I would have forgiven her. If she had done that
because she was tempted and pressed into it beyond measure,
I would have forgiven her. But she knew exactly what she was
doing and she acted willfully when she said, 'I don't want Him
any more.' Therefore, I tell you not to pray for her. I merely
showed you this so that you might see how the devil can get
hold of Christians if they will permit him to."

Then in the vision I saw a man. I didn't recognize him. Jesus
said to me, "I will show you another example of how demons
get hold of a person and how to deal with them and cast them
out."

I saw a spirit come and sit upon the man's shoulder and whis-
per in his ear. The man entertained the thoughts that Satan gave
him. Then I saw this spirit go into the man's mind. Jesus said,
"This spirit is one of the rulers of their world of the higher order.
They are the ones that always get hold of a man and eventually
possess him. There are degrees of possession, and they will bring
other evil spirits with them."

Then the Lord reminded me of the passage of Scripture in
the fifth chapter of Mark's gospel which tells about the maniac
of Gadara, and how Jesus went over the Sea of Galilee into the
country of the Gadarenes. "And when he was come out of the
ship, immediately there met him out of the tombs a man with
an unclean spirit, [Notice here that the man had just one unclean
spirit] Who had his dwelling among the tombs; and no man
could bind him, no, not with chains: Because that he had been
often bound with fetters and chains, and the chains had been
plucked asunder by him, and the fetters broken in pieces: neither
could any man tame him. And always, night and day, he was in
the mountains, and in the tombs, crying, and cutting himself with
stones. But when he saw Jesus afar off, he ran and worshipped

him, And cried with a loud voice, and said, What have I to do with thee, Jesus, thou Son of the most high God? I adjure thee by God, that thou torment me not" (Mark 5:2-7).

Notice that the spirit knew Jesus. When Jesus asked the evil spirit his name, he replied, ". . . My name is Legion, for we are many" (Mark 5:9). When Jesus cast the demons out they entered a herd of swine nearby, "and the herd ran violently down a steep place into the sea, (they were about two thousand;) and were choked in the sea" (Mark 5:13). Although only one evil spirit possessed this man from Gadara, as many as two thousand were cast out and plunged headlong into the sea after entering the herd of swine.

In the vision, the spirit got hold of the man and seemed to open his head like a trap door. Then I saw other spirits come and enter the man. Jesus said to me, "From now on when you come into the presence of anyone who is fully possessed with the devil, he will recognize you, just as the man you read about in the fifth chapter of Mark recognized Me when he came into my presence. Now walk up to this man, and, when you do, the evil spirit will recognize you."

In the vision I walked up to the man, and immediately the demon that possessed him called out, "I know you."

I said, "Yes, I realize that you know who I am, and I command you to be quiet right now in the name of Jesus."

On one occasion some people asked me to pray for a man in their family, saying that he had some kind of spells. I had never seen the man before, but when I walked into the room where he was he immediately said, "I saw you . . ." and he began to describe to me exactly when I had come into town—the street I drove down, where I went, and other facts about my arrival. I commanded him to be quiet. He obeyed, and was delivered from this evil spirit.

The Lord went on to say to me in the vision, "These spirits

will know you. Through the gift of discerning of spirits you will know what kind of spirit it is. You remember that in dealing with the man from Gadara I said, 'Come out of the man, thou unclean spirit.' I discerned it was an unclean spirit, and I commanded him to come out."

In the case of the man in the vision who had the evil spirit, I knew immediately what kind of spirit possessed him, and I commanded him to come out. But when I did so, he didn't come out.

Jesus said, "To cast them out you sometimes have to know not only the kind of spirit but also their name or number. Notice that when dealing with the man from Gadara, I said, 'Come out of the man, thou unclean spirit,' but he didn't come out."

This was something I had completely overlooked in this Scripture before, but on rereading the fifth chapter of Mark I noticed that this was true. "And he [Jesus] asked him, What is thy name? And he answered, saying, My name is Legion: for we are many" (Mark 5:9).

Jesus brought another thing to my attention concerning this passage of Scripture. "If you had been present," Jesus said to me, "you would have heard what the evil spirit said, for he used the man's voice. He talked through him. When I asked him what his name was, he replied, 'My name is Legion, for we are many.' Then he begged, 'Don't send us away out of the country.' This was the first unclean spirit that possessed the man's body speaking—using the man's voice.

"Then, you will see in the twelfth verse, 'And all the devils besought him, saying, Send us into the swine, that we may enter into them' (Mark 5:12). All of the demons cried out at once. Had you been present at this time, unless you would have had the gift of discerning of spirits to see and hear in the spirit realm, you wouldn't have known what they were saying."

I knew because this gift was operating in my ministry. All of the demons besought me—all of them spoke at once. They weren't talking out loud; that is, they weren't talking as a man would speak. They were speaking in the spirit realm.

I then walked up to the man in the vision. I discerned the kind of spirit that possessed him and commanded him to come out. Nothing happened. Jesus said to ask him his number, so I said, "How many of you are in this man?"

He said, "Nineteen more besides me."

I spoke to them saying, "I command you and all nineteen of you to come out," and they came out. Then I asked the Lord, "Where do these demons go when they come out?"

"They walk through dry places seeking rest, and they find none," He said. Then I remembered the following Scripture: "When the unclean spirit is gone out of a man, he walketh through dry places, seeking rest, and findeth none. Then he saith, I will return into my house from whence I came out; and when he is come, he findeth it empty, swept, and garnished. Then goeth he, and taketh with himself seven other spirits more wicked than himself, and they enter in and dwell there: and the last state of that man is worse than the first . . ." (Matthew 12:43-45).

I asked the Lord, "Why can't we cast them into the pit and banish them from earth forever?"

"The time for this hasn't come yet. If it would have been possible when I was on earth, I would have cast them all into the pit, and there would have been just that many less for you to have to deal with. But you will remember on one occasion the demons cried out to Me saying, '. . . What have we to do with thee, Jesus, thou Son of God? art thou come hither to torment us before the time' (Matthew 8:29)? You see, their time hasn't come yet. The time is coming when Satan and all his demons will be cast into the lake of fire where they will be forever."

While Jesus was talking to me, an evil spirit ran up between me and Jesus and spread out something that looked like a cloud or a smoke screen. I couldn't see Jesus anymore. Then the demon began to jump up and down, waving his arms and legs and yelling in a shrill voice, "Yackety, yack, yack, yack." I paused for a moment. I could hear the voice of Jesus as He continued to talk to me, but I could not understand what He was saying. I could hear His voice, but could not distinguish the words.

I thought to myself, "Doesn't the Lord know that I am missing what He is saying? I need to get that, it is important, but I am missing out on it." I wondered why Jesus didn't command the evil spirit to stop. I waited for a few more minutes. Jesus continued talking as if He didn't even know that the evil spirit was present. I wondered why the Lord didn't cast him out, but He didn't.

Finally, I grew tired of it. I pointed my finger at the evil spirit and said, "I command you in the name of Jesus Christ to be quiet!" He stopped immediately and fell to the floor. The black smoke screen disappeared and I could see Jesus once again. The evil spirit lay on the floor whimpering and whining like a whipped pup. I said, "Not only must you be quiet, but get up and get out of here." He got up and ran away.

I was still wondering why Jesus had not stopped this evil spirit from interfering as he did, and of course Jesus knew what I was thinking. He said, "If you hadn't done something about that, I couldn't have."

"Lord, I know I misunderstood You. You said You *couldn't* do anything about it, but You really meant that You *wouldn't*."

"No," He said, "if you hadn't done something about that spirit, I couldn't."

"But, Lord, You can do anything. To say that You couldn't is different from anything I ever heard preached or that I ever preached myself. That really upends my theology."

"Sometimes your theology needs upending," the Lord answered.

I said, "Lord, even though I am seeing You with my own eyes, even though I hear Your voice speaking to me as plainly as any voice I have ever heard, I cannot accept that unless You will prove it to me by the Word of God. For the Word says, '. . . In the mouth of two or three witnesses shall every word be established' (2 Corinthians 13:1). I will not accept any vision; I will not accept any revelation, if it cannot be proven by the Bible."

Instead of becoming angry with me for saying this, Jesus smiled sweetly and said, "I will give you not just two or three witnesses, I will give you four witnesses."

I said, "I have read through the New Testament one hundred and fifty times; many portions of it more than that. If that is in there, I don't know it."

"Son, there is a lot in there that you don't know," the Lord pointed out. "There is not one single place in the New Testament where believers are ever told to pray against the devil and that I will do anything about him. There is not one instance in any of the epistles written to the churches that has said to tell God to rebuke the devil. People who are praying against the devil and are asking God to rebuke the devil or do something about the devil are wasting their time. In fact, God has done all He is going to do about the devil, for the time being, until the angel comes down from heaven and takes the chain and binds him and puts him into the bottomless pit.

"Every writer of the New Testament, in writing to the church, always told the believer to do something about the devil. The believer has to have authority over the devil or the Bible wouldn't tell him to do something about the devil. 'All power [or authority] is given unto me in heaven and in earth. Go ye therefore, and teach all nations, baptizing them in the name of the Father, and of the Son, and of the Holy Ghost: Teaching them to observe all things whatsoever I have commanded you:

and, lo, I am with you alway, even unto the end of the world'
(Matthew 28:18-20).

"You might say, 'But you could have done something about
that spirit because this Scripture says you have all power and
authority in heaven and in earth.' However, I have delegated
my authority on the earth to the church. . . . 'Go ye into all
the world, and preach the gospel to every creature. He that believeth and is baptized shall be saved; but he that believeth not
shall be damned. And these signs shall follow them that believe;
In my name shall they cast out devils; they shall speak with new
tongues; They shall take up serpents; and if they drink any
deadly thing, it shall not hurt them; they shall lay hands on the
sick, and they shall recover' (Mark 16:15-18).

"One of the first signs mentioned as following believers is that
they should cast out devils. That means that in my name they
will exercise authority over the devil. I delegated my authority
over the devil to the church, and I can work only through the
church, for I am the head of the church.

"In writing to believers, James said, '. . . Resist the devil,
and he will flee from you' (James 4:7). James didn't say to get
God to resist the devil for you. He said, 'Resist the devil . . . .'
You resist the devil and he will flee from you."

I looked up the word "flee" in the dictionary later and saw
that one definition is, "To flee from as in terror." As I read that
I remembered how the evil spirits had fled in the vision when
I rebuked them. And since then I have seen them quake and
quiver in fear as I exercised my God-given authority over them.
They were not afraid of me, but rather of Jesus, whom I rep-
resented.

Jesus went on to say, "James told believers to 'Resist the devil,
and he will flee from you.' You couldn't resist the devil if you
didn't have power and authority over him.

"Peter said, 'Be sober, be vigilant; because your adversary the

devil, as a roaring lion, walketh about, seeking whom he may
devour' (1 Peter 5:8). What are you going to do? Throw up
your hands and say, 'I am whipped!'? No—a thousand times no!
We read on in verse nine, 'Whom resist stedfast in the faith . . .'
As I have said, you couldn't resist the devil if you didn't have
authority over him. But you do have authority over him and
that is the reason you can resist him.

"Paul said in his writings to the church at Ephesus, 'Neither
give place to the devil' (Ephesians 4:27). This means that you
are not to give the devil any place in you. He cannot take any
place unless you give him permission to do so. And you would
have to have authority over him or this wouldn't be true."

Then Jesus said to me, "Here are your four witnesses: I am
the first, James is the second, Peter is the third, and Paul is the
fourth. These are the four witnesses I told you I would give instead of just two or three. This establishes the fact that the believer has authority on earth, for I have delegated my authority
to you on the earth over the devil. If you don't do anything
about it, then nothing will be done." And that is why many times
nothing is done.

Then I said, "Lord, You have only told me about three catego-
ries of evil spirits: the rulers of the darkness of this world, the
powers, and the principalities. What about the wicked spirits
in the heavenlies?"

He said, "You take care of the ones on earth. I will take care
of those in the heavenlies." Jesus then exhorted me to be faithful,
saying, "Fulfill your ministry, be faithful, for the time is short,"
and He disappeared.

Then I realized that I was still on my knees in the kitchen of
that parsonage, and about an hour and a half had passed while
I was caught up in that vision.

5

I Have Come to Answer Your Prayer

It was nearly five years later when the Lord appeared to me again in what was my fourth vision of Him.

My wife and I had just returned to our home in Garland, Texas, after spending fifteen months in meetings in the state of California. We then held a meeting for our home church, the First Assembly of God in Garland. It was during the third week of this meeting that I had another supernatural visitation from the Lord.

At the close of my message one night a spirit of prayer descended upon the congregation and we all gathered around the altar to pray. We prayed for quite some time with a real burden of intercession and prayer.

After awhile I got off my knees and sat down on the steps leading from the platform. I was sitting there with my eyes open, singing in other tongues as the spirit gave utterance, when suddenly I saw Jesus standing about three feet in front of me. He said, "I have come to answer your prayer."

I knew exactly what He was talking about, as I had been praying for sometime for my wife, before leaving California, as she had a goiter. It was growing larger and larger until now she was having choking spells. One night while we were sleeping in our house trailer in California I was awakened. I saw my wife as she was just about to go out the door. I rose up and took hold of her. Immediately I saw that she didn't know what she was doing. I got her to lie back down. She later said that she didn't realize actually what had happened. When she fell back asleep, I lay there praying.

From the time that we were first married I had sensed in my spirit that she would die at an early age, and I thought perhaps that this time was approaching. I prayed the rest of the night about this and said to the Lord, "I have obeyed You and have done Your will. I left my church and my family, and have been in the evangelistic field for many years. My wife stayed at home and was faithful to raise our children. I am still a young man (at that time I was in my thirties), and we have been married for many years. Please let me keep my wife."

In the vision the Lord said to me, "I have come to answer that prayer. Tell your wife to be operated on, for she will live and not die."

Although I didn't mention it to my wife, I had felt all along that if she were operated on she would die. She later told me that she had known for several years that she would die when she was operated on for this goiter.

But the Lord said to me, "She will live and not die. It was divine destiny that she would die, but I have heard your prayers and have come to answer them. She shall live."

Then Jesus said something that absolutely melted me and I have never been able to forget it. It blessed and helped me then and it still blesses me. He said, "I did this, Son, just because you asked me to. You don't know how I long to do for my children if they would only ask Me and believe Me. Many times they beg and cry and pray, but they don't believe. And I cannot answer their prayers unless they have faith, because I cannot violate my

Word. But how often I long to help them if only they would let Me by taking Me at my Word and bringing Me their problems, trusting Me to undertake for them." Again He said, "Tell your wife to be operated on, for she will live and not die." With those words He disappeared.

And even though the doctors were greatly concerned about my wife's condition, she and I had great joy through it all because we knew the outcome in advance.

6

The Angel's Visit

My fifth vision occurred in Port Neches, Texas, in January, 1958, while I was holding a revival meeting in the First Assembly of God Church. One night, as we were praying around the altar, a great spirit of prayer and intercession seemed to come upon the whole church. We prayed together for quite some time, and then I got up and sat in a chair on the platform. I was sitting there with my eyes open singing in other tongues.

Suddenly the Lord Jesus appeared on the platform, and about three feet behind him stood an angel. Jesus said to me, "I sent my angel to speak to you nearly a year ago out in California."

I remembered the occasion, and that I had not responded to him. One afternoon I was lying across the bed in my house trailer resting. I was meditating and reading my Bible, getting ready for the service that evening. Suddenly I had the feeling that someone had come into the trailer. I looked but couldn't see anybody. But I was positive that someone had come in through the door. It even seemed as if I had heard the door open and close. I sensed that someone came and stood beside the bed. I reached out my hand to feel whatever might be there and I said, "I know you are there. Who are you?"

There was no response. Although I never saw anyone, I sensed that someone stood there for a few moments, then turned around, retraced his steps around the foot of the bed, went up through the trailer, and out the door.

Then I seemed to be led of the spirit to open my Bible and read about the ministry of angels. I felt that an angel had come to me, but I had not opened my heart to this visitation.

We continued our ministry in the state of California. The children were traveling with us at this time, doing their school work through correspondence courses which we helped them with. As they had been traveling with us for about a year, we decided that it was just too hard on them. They were doing a great deal of traveling, were in two services a day, as well as trying to keep up with their studies by correspondence. Therefore, we decided to return to our home in Garland so that the children could attend the public schools.

The people who had been renting our house moved out so that we could move in. But we had sold all our furniture when we bought the house trailer, so we had to buy a whole house full of new furniture. Of course, we had to go in debt to do so. This made our monthly payments extremely high, as we were still making payments on the trailer, the house, the car, and then the furniture—not to mention our living expenses.

For more than a year we lacked about $100 every month in getting enough money to meet our budget. Therefore, we had to go in debt that much. I had to borrow $100 each month just to pay expenses and keep operating.

Back in 1956 the Lord had spoken to me warning me that a recession was coming—not a depression but a recession—and that I should prepare for it. The recession did come in 1957. Then fifteen months later, when the Lord appeared to me in the vision in Port Neches, Texas, I was still bearing the consequences of my not getting ready for the recession.

The Lord said to me, "I sent my angel to warn you again when you were out in California, because I saw that you hadn't listened to the leading of my Spirit and didn't respond to the warning. If you had yielded to this spirit [because we can't see angels with the natural eye unless God so wills, for they are spirits], and if you had responded to the Holy Spirit, then you would have been able to see into the realm of the spirit. By the discerning of spirits you would have seen the angel and he would have delivered his message to you. If you would have received it, you would have been spared all of this financial trouble." As fifteen months had passed since this time, and I was going in debt each month for $100, this now totaled a debt of $1,500.

The Lord continued, "I am going to help you, however, with your finances." And He did help me. We had been trying to sell the house trailer, but as the new ten-foot-wide models had just come on the market, it seemed no one would buy our eight-foot-wide trailer. But with the Lord's help, it was sold within a month.

He also said, "I am going to help you in your ministry as well," and He talked to me further about my ministry, admonishing me to be faithful. Then pointing to the angel standing beside Him He said, "This is your angel."

"My angel?" I said.

"Yes, your angel, and if you will respond to him, he will appear to you as I will at times; and will give you guidance and direction concerning the things of life, for angels are ministering spirits who are sent to minister for those who are the heirs of salvation."

Everything that the Lord had shown to me in this vision concerning my finances and my ministry came to pass within ninety days.

7

A Hospital Visitor

The sixth time that the Lord appeared to me was in February, 1959, while I was conducting a revival meeting in El Paso, Texas.

I slipped and fell on my right elbow, hurting my arm rather severely. At first I thought it was broken, and as this was about nine-thirty at night I went to the hospital to have a doctor look at it and set the bones, if necessary.

While we were riding along in the car, about a block away from the hospital, the Lord spoke to me and told me that my arm was not broken, but that I had a fracture and had knocked my elbow out of place. The Lord also said that this was the devil's work, but that He would make it turn out for His glory and work for my good. He also told me that He would talk to me about it later, and that I should not fear or worry about anything.

At the hospital the doctor X-rayed my arm and confirmed what I already knew to be true, as the Lord had told me on the way to the hospital. The doctor explained that my elbow was knocked out of place and that there were some chips off the bone. This, he explained, was even worse than a broken arm because the ligaments and muscles that hold the elbow in place had to be put back in place. He would have to give me an anesthetic to do this, he said; otherwise I would not be able to stand the pain. Then he said that I would have to be in the hospital for a couple of days. After that I would have to wear a cast on my arm for at least four weeks and then carry it in a sling for awhile after that.

The next afternoon I was propped up in bed in my hospital room. I was fully dressed as I sat there, for I had been walking up and down the hospital corridors. I had gone to sit in the lobby for awhile, and then my dinner tray was brought to me. After I finished dinner, I was all alone and feeling rather lonesome.

Then I heard footsteps coming down the corridor toward my room. I looked toward the door to see who was coming to see me, as it was just six-thirty and too early for visitors. Someone dressed in white came through the door and I supposed it to be a nurse. As I looked closer I saw it was Jesus. It seemed as if my hair stood straight up on end. Cold chill bumps popped out all over my body, and I couldn't say a word.

Jesus approached my bed and sat down on a chair. He seemed robed in white and had some sort of sandals on. Previously when I had seen Him His feet were bare.

The Lord began His conversation with me by saying, "I told you in the automobile the other night as you approached the hospital that your arm was not broken, and you have since learned that this is true. I also told you that I would talk to you about this later."

Someone might ask how the Lord told me this. While riding along in the car I heard the Word of the Lord speaking so clearly to me that I thought everyone in the car had heard it also. In fact, I asked, "Did you hear that?" of those riding with me. But no one else heard anything.

In the Old Testament we read the expression over and over,

". . . the word of the Lord came unto me saying . . ." (Jeremiah 2:1). Or it might say ". . . and the word of the Lord came unto him saying . . ." (1 Kings 17:2). This Word certainly wasn't audible, for if it had been an audible voice like the human voice speaking, everyone present would have heard it. The prophet would not have had to tell the people what the Lord said. But the Word wasn't audible, it came to the prophet's spirit from the Spirit of God—the Holy Ghost. It is so real that it seems audible at the time, for it was so real to me I thought everyone with me in the car had heard it too.

In my hospital room, the Lord reminded me of what He had told me the other night in the car on the way to the hospital. "I told you that your arm was not broken but that you had knocked your elbow out of place and had had a slight fracture. I also told you that this was the devil's work, but that it would all work out to my glory and for your good."

I replied, "Yes, Lord, and I haven't worried about it for a minute, for I knew what You had told me. In fact, I have just been having a glorious time in the Lord."

"You are to be commended for taking Me at my word," He went on. "Now I want to say this to you. This has happened to you, not because it was my perfect will, for this is not my will at all. However, this has happened because you got out of my perfect will into my permissive will." He reminded me of the Scripture, "And be not conformed to this world: but be ye transformed by the renewing of your mind, that ye may prove what is that good, and acceptable, and perfect, will of God" (Romans 12:2). I read somewhere another translation of this verse which reads, ". . . that you may prove what is that good, and permissive, and perfect will of God." The word "permissive" in this translation is used instead of the word "acceptable."

The Lord explained that He permits people to do things that aren't expressly His will. For example, He said, "It wasn't my will that Israel have a king, and I told them so. But they wanted to be like other nations. They kept clamoring for a king, and so God permitted them to have a king.

"Some time ago you were preaching to a convention of ministers, and you stated that your ministry was that of a prophet and a teacher. You have gotten into trouble because you have reversed the order and have put your teaching ministry first and your prophetic ministry second. When you did that, you got out of my perfect will into my permissive will, thus opening the door for the devil to attack you.

"You might ask why, if I knew that you were going to fall and hurt your arm, I didn't prevent it. I could have, of course, but I didn't want to. And instead of your being angry with me for not preventing it, you should be glad that I allowed it to happen. If I hadn't permitted Satan to do this to arrest your attention, you would not have lived past the age of fifty-five because you would have continued in my permissive will instead of my perfect will.

"This is the third time I have had to speak to you about this. For this reason, I am going to let you wear your arm in a cast and then in a sling for a little while. I will speed up the healing process, however, so that you will not be disabled as long as the doctor has said would be necessary." Then He told me exactly the day I would get out of the cast.

He went on to say, "You have enjoyed divine health for twenty-five years now. Even now you are not sick." (The Lord had kept me from sickness and accidents for all that time. Thirty-seven years have now passed in which the Lord has kept me from sickness and has given me divine health. This is the only accident I have had in all this time.) "But," He said, "you have been out of my perfect will for two years and have been walking in my permissive will only."

Although I had been anointed by the spirit for the ministry of a prophet and teacher, I had been putting my teaching ministry first because I like to teach. That was my natural preference. I had seen a great need for Bible teaching, and, of course, pastors encouraged my teaching ministry. But the Lord told me in this vision that I was going to have to reverse it and put my prophet's ministry first.

I realized that this accident was not caused by the Lord, but that He merely permitted it to happen. "The thief cometh not, but for to steal, and to kill, and to destroy: I am come that they might have life and that they might have it more abundantly" (John 10:10). That which steals and destroys is the enemy. The Lord doesn't commission it, although He may permit it. For instance, God didn't cause Job's children to be killed or his flocks stolen. God didn't cause the thieves to rob him or the fire to burn his crops. God didn't smite his body with boils. The devil did it, but the Lord permitted him to do it.

In order to get my attention and to bring about my complete submission and obedience to His perfect will, God had allowed this calamity to come into my life. He said to me, "It is my perfect will that men and women enjoy divine healing and divine health, but many are like you and are living in only my permissive will. For that reason, difficulties have been permitted to come their way. Others are weak in faith. Their faith is not strong enough to appropriate the healing that belongs to them. Some don't even know what belongs to them. Always pray for these people who are sick and in the hospitals and are under the care of doctors that I will speed up the healing process, for I will do that for you."

Thirteen days later I went back to the doctor to have my cast changed. When it was removed the doctor looked at my arm in amazement and said, "I have never seen an arm heal so rapidly." Normally it would have taken four weeks for my arm to heal properly.

The doctor had previously told my wife that I would never be able to touch my shoulder with that arm. However, I can. The Lord told me as He sat there by my hospital bed that He would restore 99 percent of the use of that arm. He said He was going to leave that 1 percent disability to remind me not to disobey Him again, but to use the ministry He had given me. (My arm gives me only the slightest amount of trouble. No one can ever tell that anything is wrong, and most of the time I have no difficulty with it.)

As the Lord continued to speak to me in the vision, He talked to me about the healing ministry, about divine healing, and divine health. He reminded me of His promise to Israel, ". . . If thou wilt diligently hearken to the voice of the Lord thy God, and wilt do that which is right in His sight, and wilt give ear to His commandments, and keep all His statutes, I will put none of these diseases upon thee, which I have brought upon the Egyptians: for I am the Lord that healeth thee" (Exodus 15:26), and also "And the Lord will take away from thee all sickness . . ." (Deuteronomy 7:15), and ". . . the number of thy days I will fulfill" (Exodus 23:26).

Speaking to me that night in the vision, the Lord said, "Israel was not born again, they were not the church in the same sense that you are. You have become children of God, actually the sons of God. 'But as many as received him, to them gave he power to become the sons of God, even to them that believe on his name' (John 1:12). 'Behold, what manner of love the Father hath bestowed upon us, that we should be called the sons of God . . . Beloved, now are we the sons of God . . .' (1 John 3:1, 2).

"The Israelites were not my sons, they were my servants. And if it was not my will that my servants should be sick, certainly it is not my will that my sons should be sick. I have provided healing for them.

"I am going to talk to you now about the prophet's ministry," He said. "You have missed it and have only been in my permissive will because you have reversed the order, putting the teaching ministry first and the prophet's ministry second. Did you ever notice in my Word that everywhere the ministry is mentioned, the prophet's ministry is mentioned first and the teaching ministry second? 'Wherefore he saith, When he ascended up on high, he led captivity captive, and gave gifts unto men . . . And he gave some apostles; and some, prophets; and some, evangelists; and some, pastors and teachers; For the perfecting of the saints, for the work of the ministry, for the edifying of the body of Christ' (Ephesians 4:8, 11, 12).

"These are the ministry gifts which Paul said God gave to men. And He gave them for this purpose: 'For the perfecting of the saints, for the work of the ministry, for the edifying of the body of Christ.'

"Notice the order. Apostles are mentioned first. There are some who say that there were only the twelve original apostles. However, there are twenty-four individuals in the New Testament who are called apostles. The Greek word for 'apostle' means 'the sent one.' Even Paul himself was not an apostle in the sense of being one of the original twelve, for he was not with them from the beginning of my earthly ministry. Judas was one of the twelve original apostles, but after the betrayal he went out and hanged himself and was replaced by Matthias. This made Matthias the thirteenth apostle.

"'Which when the apostles, Barnabas and Paul . . .' (Acts 14:14). Notice that according to this verse Barnabas was just as much an apostle as Paul was, making them the fourteenth and fifteenth apostles.

"In Galatians we read that Paul said, 'Neither went I up to Jerusalem to them which were apostles before me; but I went into Arabia, and returned again unto Damascus. Then after three years I went up to Jerusalem to see Peter, and abode with him fifteen days. But other of the apostles saw I none, save James the Lord's brother' (Galatians 1:17-19). Here Paul calls James an apostle, although he was not one of the original twelve. James was sent to be the head of the church at Jerusalem. Paul calls him an apostle because he was a 'sent one.' This makes James the sixteenth apostle mentioned in the Scriptures.

"In Romans Paul wrote, 'Salute Andronicus and Junia, my kinsmen, and my fellowprisoners, who are of note among the apostles, who also were in Christ before me' (Romans 16:7). Therefore, Andronicus and Junia were apostles number seventeen and eighteen.

"Paul began his epistle to the Thessalonians, 'Paul, and Silvanus, and Timotheus, unto the church of the Thessalonians . . . in God . . .' (1 Thessalonians 1:1). Then writing in the second chapter he refers to the three of them as the apostles of Christ. This would make these three men apostles number nineteen, twenty, and twenty-one.

"In 2 Corinthians 8:23 two unnamed brethren are called apostles, raising the number to twenty-three apostles.

"In Philippians Paul said, 'Yet I supposed it necessary to send to you Epaphroditus, my brother, and companion in labour, and fellowsoldier, but your messenger, and he that ministered to my wants' (Philippians 2:25). The Greek word used in this text for messenger is the same one that is translated 'apostle' elsewhere. Therefore, this makes twenty-four apostles mentioned in the New Testament."

We can see from this that a person can be a "sent one" or a messenger of the church and rightly be called an apostle of the church. Smith Wigglesworth was called an apostle of faith. When Christ calls and sends someone, he is an apostle of Christ.

There is no mention of missionaries among the ministry gifts listed in Ephesians: "And he gave some, apostles; and some, prophets; and some, evangelists; and some, pastors and teachers"

(Ephesians 4:11). In fact, the word "missionary" is not found in the New Testament. The ministry of a missionary is involved in the calling of an apostle. It is a ministry, but not necessarily an office. A person doesn't have the office of an apostle, he has the ministry of one. For example, if someone were called by the Holy Spirit to be a missionary to Africa, a missionary committee might send him out, but if he were really sent out by the Holy Spirit, he would be an apostle to the people of Africa. As Jesus pointed out to me in the vision, neither Paul nor Barnabas were apostles to begin with, "Now there were in the church that was at Antioch certain prophets and teachers; as Barnabas, and Simeon that was called Niger, and Lucius of Cyrene, and Manaen, which had been brought up with Herod the tetrarch, and Saul" (Acts 13:1). All five of these men were prophets and/or teachers. Saul and Barnabas were mentioned here, but they were not called apostles at all. They were called prophets and teachers. We do know that Paul was a prophet and a teacher. We are told that Barnabas was a teacher.

Later they became apostles. "As they ministered to the Lord, and fasted, the Holy Ghost said, Separate me Barnabas and Saul for the work whereunto I have called them. And when they had fasted and prayed, and laid their hands on them, they sent them away. So they, being sent forth by the Holy Ghost, departed . . ." (Acts 13:2-4). In other words, Paul and Barnabas were "sent ones," or apostles.

The next chapter in the book of Acts tells us, "Which when the apostles, Barnabas and Paul . . ." (Acts 14:14). Barnabas was called an apostle because he was a "sent one" or an apostle to the Gentiles as much as Paul was.

The reason I discuss these things here is that the Lord brought these thoughts out to me in the vision to show me that the apostle's ministry is still for us today, as is the prophet's ministry. In dealing with me about the prophet's ministry coming first and the teaching ministry second, He pointed out that the prophet's ministry is listed above the teaching ministry in the Scriptures. Paul listed them in the order of their importance. "And he gave some, apostles; and some, prophets; and some, evangelists; and some, pastors and teachers" (Ephesians 4:11).

In the Scripture in Acts 13:1 where it mentions the ministers who were praying at the church in Antioch, it doesn't say "teachers and prophets." It says "prophets and teachers," and goes on to list them.

As Jesus sat in the chair by my hospital bed, He pointed out to me the following Scripture: "Now ye are the body of Christ, and members in particular. And God hath set some in the church, first apostles, secondarily prophets, thirdly teachers, after that miracles, then gifts of healings, helps, governments, diversities of tongues. Are all apostles? are all prophets? are all teachers? are all workers of miracles? Have all the gifts of healing? do all speak with tongues? do all interpret" (1 Corinthians 12:27-30)?

Here, again, Paul was talking about ministry gifts, not spiritual gifts. Notice too that the prophet's ministry is again listed before the teaching ministry. Every time these gifts are mentioned, the prophet's ministry is mentioned first.

"This is the reason you have gotten into trouble," the Lord said to me. "You have put the teaching ministry first and the prophet's ministry last. When you did that, you got out of my perfect will and into only my permissive will."

He went on to talk to me about the ministry of the prophet. A prophet is one, He explained, who has visions and revelations. Notice that Paul is called a prophet and teacher in Acts 13:1. In the Old Testament, a prophet was called a seer because he saw and knew things supernaturally.

"Let the prophets speak two or three, and let the other judge. If any thing be revealed to another that sitteth by, let the first hold his peace" (1 Corinthians 14:29, 30). Here we see that a prophet is one who has visions and revelations; that is, things are revealed unto him. Paul said that he was taught the gospel by revelation of Jesus Christ. It all came by revelation. Man didn't teach it to him. A prophet is one who sees and knows things supernaturally because he has revelation gifts, plus the gift of prophecy operating in his life and ministry that constitute the office of a prophet.

A man is first called to be a minister. In other words, the calling of God is upon his life. He may preach or teach, or be in the ministry in some capacity. To be an evangelist is a calling. The teaching ministry is a calling. To be a pastor is a calling. And to be a prophet is a calling. But in order to be a prophet he must also have at least two of the revelation gifts, as well as the gift of prophecy, operating in his ministry. The revelation gifts, as Jesus pointed out to me, are the word of wisdom, the word of knowledge, and the gift of discerning of spirits.

To stand in the office of a prophet, one is first of all a minister of the gospel separated and called to the ministry with the calling of God upon his life. Secondly, he has at least two of these revelation gifts—the word of wisdom, the word of knowledge, or the discerning of spirits, plus the gift of prophecy.

After I received the baptism of the Holy Spirit, the word of knowledge immediately began to operate in my life, and ever since then it has continued to be manifested. Since then, when I am in the spirit, the gift of discerning of spirits is also in operation. Therefore, the word of knowledge and the discerning of spirits, plus prophecy are operating in my ministry when I am in the spirit. This constitutes the office of a prophet.

Any layman might receive a word of knowledge occasionally. The spiritual gift of the word of knowledge is a supernatural revelation by the Holy Spirit of certain facts in the mind of God. God knows everything but He doesn't reveal everything that He knows. He just gives a person a "word" of knowledge. A word is a fragmentary part of a sentence. He gives an individual what He wants him to know at the time, just part of the knowledge that He has. It is something that is given by the Holy Ghost.

Jesus pointed all of this out to me as He sat by my bedside and spoke to me. He said that any person, whether he is a prophet, minister or layman, might have the word of knowledge occasionally. Something might be revealed to him as he might need it. But even the layman is not called to minister. The minister may be an evangelist or a pastor, but he wouldn't be called a prophet. He may get the word of knowledge to help someone, but that doesn't make him a prophet. That manifestation just comes at the moment to meet a certain need.

Any spirit-filled person, whether layman or minister, may need a word of wisdom occasionally, and this gift might be manifested then. But to constitute the prophet's office there has to be a continued manifestation of at least two of these gifts—the word of knowledge, the word of wisdom, the discerning of spirits—plus prophecy.

Jesus pointed out that in the Old Testament all the gifts were in operation except tongues and interpretation of tongues. "Tongues," He said, "are exclusive with this dispensation." Old Testament prophets knew things supernaturally. One example of this is found in the fifth chapter of 2 Kings. When Naaman, a captain in the army of the king of Syria, was healed of leprosy after dipping seven times in the River Jordan, as commanded by the prophet Elisha, he offered Elisha much silver and gold. However, Elisha refused to accept Naaman's money because he realized that Naaman was trying to pay for his healing. And it cannot be purchased—it is a gift from God.

Elisha had a servant named Gehazi, and he went after Naaman, telling him the story that two young prophets had come to Elisha, and although Elisha wouldn't take anything for himself, he had said it would be all right to take some talents of silver and gold and some changes of raiment for these young prophets. Naaman was so thrilled and thankful for his healing that he gave Gehazi twice as much as he had asked for.

Gehazi was lying, of course. He had made up the story about the two young prophets. He took Naaman's gifts and hid them for his own use. Then when he went into the presence of Elisha, the prophet asked him where he had been. Gehazi lied and said, "Nowhere."

Elisha said, ". . . Went not mine heart with thee, when the man turned again from his chariot to meet thee . . ." (2 Kings 5:26)? He knew the truth in his spirit. This had to be a supernatural revelation. It was the operation of the word of knowledge in the office of the prophet.

Many people think that if one has this ministry he can automatically tell everything about everybody. But the gift operates only as the Lord wills. We can't just turn it on and off as we wish. Gehazi was with the prophet all the time and he knew that Elisha didn't know everything all the time. This is the reason he probably thought that he could get away with his deceit.

People often write to me wanting me to tell them what is wrong with them. However, a person has to be with me in a service when the gift is operating. I can't just push a button and start operating like a tape recorder. It is as the spirit wills and His anointing comes on me.

It is for this reason that I preach about it, for then the faith of the congregation rises and the anointing comes upon me to begin ministering. If I could minister that way every night I would do it. At times God has had me prophesy to every single person in the crowd, giving me an individual message for everyone. Where the spirit is in manifestation, anything can happen. I cannot make it happen, though, just because I want it to happen.

Once while I was preaching in Kansas, a minister's wife asked me to pray for her. As she spoke, the revelation started coming to me and I told her to wait a minute. I said, "If you tell me your needs and then I tell you what the Lord has shown me, you wouldn't know but what I had spoken from my own knowledge. But when God supernaturally tells me a person's need and then gives instruction how to solve the problem, then that person knows it is supernatural."

In this instance, the Word of the Lord came unto me showing me that a little while after this woman was saved she had sinned. Ever since then, a deceiving devil had troubled her and told her repeatedly that she had committed the unpardonable sin. The Lord showed me this woman in a vision. I saw her very depressed and discouraged. I said to her, "I can see you for two and three weeks at a time with your shades pulled down in your home, lying in bed with a damp cloth on your head because your head hurts so much." She was amazed that I could know this. Then I gave her the message that God gave to me, how that the Lord had shown me she had committed a sin shortly after she was saved, and that since then the devil had tormented her mind with doubt and discouragement.

She told me that two years after she was saved she told a lie, and that the devil had tormented her ever since. She told me how these spirits of depression would come upon her for three weeks at a time and she would shut herself up in her room with a cool, damp cloth on her head to ease the pain. I took authority over this deceiving spirit and commanded him to leave her at once. Since then I have seen her again and learned that she has not been troubled since I ministered to her.

In another city I prayed for a young man who was having epileptic seizures. He was old enough to serve in the Army, but he was rejected because of these seizures. When he came into the healing line, I knew by the revelation of the Holy Ghost (the word of knowledge) that I had to deal with the spirit, so I cast out the spirit in Jesus' name.

Twelve months later I was back in that church for one service. As I walked through a side door and sat down on the platform, my eyes fell on this young man. The Word of the Lord came to me and brought me the word of knowledge saying, "Last year when you were here you cast that evil spirit out of his body. For twelve months he has not had an epileptic seizure. However, in the last two weeks he has had three seizures in the night while sleeping, and he has been awakened by them." Before this time the boy had never had a seizure at night. Then the Word went on to say to me, "The reason for these seizures is that he went to bed fearful and went to sleep afraid."

The Lord then told me that before I preached I should call this boy to the platform and tell him what the Lord had just shown me. Then He said I should command the spirit to leave again. I was also to teach the boy how to resist fear and maintain his healing. As I obeyed the Lord and called him to the front, telling him all that the Lord had shown me, the boy was amazed and verified what I said.

I told him that I was going to cast that spirit out of him, but that when he was alone he would be on his own and would have to resist that devil, as we are told to do in James 4:7. Many years have passed since that time, and he has never had another epileptic seizure.

Manifested in this boy's case was a combination of the gifts of the word of knowledge, discerning of spirits, plus prophecy and a teaching ministry that taught him how to resist the devil and maintain what he had. In dealing with me about this ministry of a prophet, the Lord covered these different manifestations or functions of this office. Here I merely give some illustrations to help them to be more easily understood.

The Word of God tells us that He gave some apostles, some prophets, some evangelists, some pastors, and some teachers, as we have already seen in Ephesians 4:11. Some may say, "Yes, but these ministries have been done away with now and the only ministries that we have today are teachers, pastors, and evangelists. There are no apostles or prophets today." But notice here that Paul made no distinction. He said that God called some apostles, some prophets, some evangelists, some pastors, and some teachers. And for what purpose? "For the perfecting of the saints, for the work of the ministry, for the edifying of the body of Christ" (Ephesians 4:12). Have the saints all been perfected yet? Is there any work of the ministry going on today? Does the body of Christ need edifying? Then all of these ministries and ministry gifts should be in operation. They haven't been done away with.

We need to find our place in God's plan and know what He has called us to do, for He will equip us by His Spirit to stand in the office for which He has called us. We can use the ministry gifts that He has given us to minister according to His will, purpose, and plan.

As I said, from the moment that I was baptized with the Holy Ghost and spoke in other tongues, the word of knowledge immediately began to be manifest in my life, and the Lord mentioned that to me in the vision as He sat by my bedside. The word of knowledge, He pointed out, is supernatural revelation, as all gifts of the spirit are supernatural. If one of them is supernatural, then all of them are supernatural. If the word of knowledge is not a supernatural revelation, then the gift of healing would not be supernatural.

Notice, too, that it isn't called the "gift of knowledge." It is the gift of "the word of knowledge." The spiritual gift of the word of knowledge is a supernatural revelation by the Holy Ghost concerning people, places, or things in the present or in the past. The word of wisdom concerns the knowledge of the future. The word of wisdom is a supernatural revelation concerning the plan and purpose of God.

When the word of knowledge began to operate in my life after I was filled with the Holy Ghost, I would know things supernaturally about people, places, and things. Sometimes I would know through a vision. Sometimes while I was preaching, a cloud would appear and my eyes would be opened so that I would see a vision concerning someone in the congregation. In the vision I would see this person in another town, and I would see the sin that he had committed there. Then I would tell him about it— never publicly, for the Bible teaches that only hypocrites should be rebuked publicly. Usually these people are not hypocrites, even though they have sinned. They want to do right. They want to serve God. God shows these things many times to help them and to show them how to overcome temptation. We need to realize that this kind of ministry is Scriptural and is necessary today.

Sometimes the word of knowledge comes in a vision, sometimes by an inward revelation, sometimes as the interpretation of a message in tongues or a prophecy. Sometimes it is given by tongues and interpretation. Sometimes it is spoken by prophecy.

As I have said, although one may have the word of knowledge operating in his life, that wouldn't necessarily make him a prophet. The word of knowledge and the discerning of spirits will operate in connection with prophecy many times. It is not called the gift of prophecy because the simple gift of prophecy has no revelation with it. Although it is true that any person may have a word of wisdom, a word of knowledge, or the discerning of spirits given to him occasionally, that would not make him a prophet.

"But he that prophesieth speaketh unto men to edification, and exhortation, and comfort" (1 Corinthians 14:3). The simple gift of prophecy, therefore, is not given for revelation. Very often in the prophet's ministry the utterance he gives will have revelation in it because the prophet has other gifts operating also. But the fact that one prophesies does not make him a prophet.

Many have thought that tongues and interpretation and prophecy are only for public ministry. But there is more. The simple gift of prophecy can be used as prayer in worship to God as well as in addressing the congregation or individuals. In the Book of Psalms we have a number of psalms, songs, and prayers that were given in prophecy by the Holy Spirit. They were spoken out by the inspiration of the Holy Ghost. And the Holy Ghost will help us even today in our prayer life with prophecy, and also with tongues and interpretation.

I use tongues and interpretation all the time in my prayer life. Many times I pray in tongues for an hour or so, and then pray the interpretation in English. In this way, my mind is edified as well as my spirit because "He that speaketh in an unknown tongue edifieth himself [or his spirit] . . . (1 Corinthians 14:4). If I prayed only in tongues, my spirit would be edified but my mind would be unfruitful. I have prayed as much as six hours a day in tongues and then prayed the interpretation in English. At other times, I have used prophecy entirely. None of this comes from my own mind, but I pray in English by a supernatural utterance given by the Holy Ghost. It is most blessed to use prophecy in prayer. It lifts one higher than anything because prophecy carries greater inspiration.

Praying in this manner is not limited to ministers. All spirit-filled Christians can do it. But as I have said, praying in tongues and interpretation or praying with prophecy would not in itself make the individual a prophet.

All of these things the Lord taught me as He sat beside my hospital bed that evening. Here I merely sum them up in my own words.

There are three types of revelations and three types of visions. The highest type of revelation and the lowest type of vision are very similar and sometimes an individual cannot tell the difference. First of all, there is what the Lord called a spiritual vision in which a person has a vision in his spirit, or *sees* in his spirit.

For instance, when Paul was on the road to Damascus, he was breathing out threatenings against the church, and had letters in his possession giving him authority to put all Christians in jail. As he approached the city of Damascus, suddenly a light brighter than the noonday sun shone around him. ". . . and heard a voice saying unto him, Saul, Saul, why persecutest thou me? And he said, Who art thou, Lord? And the Lord said, I am Jesus whom thou persecutest . . ." (Acts 9:4, 5).

Paul, in relating his own experience, said that when this happened his eyes were blind and could not see. Paul didn't see the Lord with his physical eyes. He saw in the spirit realm.

In this same ninth chapter of Acts it tells of how the Lord spoke to Ananias, who was just a layman in the city of Damascus. The Lord told him to go to a street called Straight and "enquire . . . for one called Saul, of Tarsus: for, behold, he prayeth, And hath seen in a vision a man named Ananias coming in, and putting his hand on him, that he might receive his sight" (verses 11, 12).

"And Ananias went his way, and entered into the house; and putting his hands on him said, Brother Saul, the Lord, even Jesus, that appeared unto thee in the way as thou camest, hath sent me . . ." (Acts 9:17).

So we see that Jesus appeared to Saul and he saw Him. But his physical eyes were blinded. This was a spiritual vision. He saw Him with the eyes of his spirit. This is the first and lowest type of vision.

Jesus pointed out to me that the second highest type of vision is when one falls into a trance. We see an example of this type of vision when Paul went to Jerusalem the first time. He said, "And it came to pass, that, when I was come again to Jerusalem, even while I prayed in the temple, I was in a trance; And saw him [Jesus] saying unto me, Make haste, and get thee quickly out of Jerusalem: for they will not receive thy testimony concerning me" (Acts 22:17, 18). Notice that Paul says he was in a trance.

The tenth chapter of Acts relates the story of Peter's vision in which the Lord told him to take the gospel to the Gentiles. Peter went up on the housetop to pray and there "fell into a trance" (verse 10).

When one falls into a trance, his physical senses are suspended for the moment. He is not aware of where he is or of anything that contacts the physical. He is not unconscious; he is just more conscious of spiritual things than he is of physical things.

When Peter fell into a trance, he ". . . saw heaven opened . . ." (verse 11). He was seeing into the spirit realm. So we see from the Bible that both Peter and Paul fell into a trance and saw into the spirit realm. A trance then is the second highest type of vision.

The third type of vision is actually the highest type and is called an open vision. When this happens, one's physical senses are not suspended. His physical eyes are not closed. He possesses all his physical capabilities, yet sees into the realm of the spirit. This is the kind of vision I had when I saw Jesus walk into my hospital room. I *heard* His footsteps. I *saw* Him enter my room just as plainly as any man I have ever seen in my life. I *saw* Him sit down beside my bed. I *heard* His voice as plainly as any man's voice I have ever heard in my life.

When the Lord dealt with me concerning my ministry and showed me about the revelation gifts which operate in my life, He spoke to me concerning prophets of the Old Testament who were called seers and knew and saw things supernaturally. The Lord reminded me of the time when Saul, as a young boy, was out looking for some of his father's donkeys that had strayed away (1 Samuel 9). When Saul inquired about them, someone suggested that he go to the prophet and ask him where to find the donkeys, for he would know where they were. Saul went to the prophet Samuel, and was told that the donkeys had been found three days before, and that now people were out looking for Saul. Samuel knew this supernaturally.

Samuel also asked Saul to wait, for he had a word of wisdom to him concerning God's plan. Saul was then anointed to be the first king of Israel. Certainly Samuel didn't know the whereabouts of every stray donkey in Israel. There could have been many stray donkeys at that time. God had a purpose in revealing this to him at that particular time, for it concerned Israel's future king.

One time I stopped to visit with a minister at the site where he was building a new church. After he showed me around, we got into our cars to leave. Just as we did, the Word of the Lord came unto me saying that I should tell this minister that he wasn't going to live much longer unless he corrected himself in three things: his diet, his money matters, and his lack of love for the brethren.

I stepped out of my car to go and tell him this, but someone else walked up to his car about that time and began to talk with him. I sat back down in my car and began to reason with myself. I knew that he probably wouldn't take this advice from me. He certainly didn't walk in love toward the brethren, and he would probably slap my face. As I sat there talking myself out of it, the minister left without my telling him what the Lord had shown me. That was the last time I saw him, for three years later he died.

Everywhere I go I read Scriptures about the ministry gifts—1 Corinthians 12:28 says that God has set these ministries in the church.

The fourteenth chapter of 1 Corinthians tells about the prophet speaking and the gifts of tongues and interpretation. "If any man speak in an unknown tongue, let it be by two, or at the most by three, and that by course; and let one interpret. But if there be no interpreter, let him keep silence in the church; and let him speak to himself, and to God. Let the prophets speak two or three, and let the other judge. If any thing be revealed to another that sitteth by, let the first hold his peace" (1 Corinthians 14:27-30).

Most Full Gospel churches will permit tongues and interpretations in the services, but many shy away from the prophet's ministry. However, it is all in the same chapter. If one should be omitted, then the other should be too. When the Lord was dealing with me as He sat by my bedside and talked with me concerning the prophet's ministry, He said that if a church doesn't accept my ministry, I should go my way, and shake the dust off my feet against them, so to speak.

The Lord told me that the time is short. The work must be done quickly in these last days. He said, "The judgment must begin in the house of God, and if the righteous scarcely be saved, where shall the sinner and the ungodly appear. If the church won't accept this ministry, then they wouldn't accept His Word." He went on to say that if a pastor would not accept this message, then judgment would come on him. The Lord said that if He gave me a message or a revelation to a pastor, I should deliver it. If He gives me a message for a church or for an individual, then I am to deliver it.

Some do not believe that personal prophecy is Scriptural. They do not believe that a prophet may have a message for an individual. However, Luke says, "And the next day we that were of Paul's company departed, and came unto Caesarea: and we entered into the house of Philip the evangelist, which was one of the seven; and abode with him. And the same man had four daughters, virgins, which did prophesy. And as we tarried there many days, there came down from Judea a certain prophet, named

Agabus. And when he was come unto us, he took Paul's girdle, and bound his own hands and feet, and said, Thus saith the Holy Ghost, So shall the Jews at Jerusalem bind the man that owneth this girdle, and shall deliver him into the hands of the Gentiles" (Acts 21:8-11).

One phase of the prophet's ministry is that he speaks for God. In the Scripture quoted above, Agabus didn't tell Paul not to go to Jerusalem. He merely told him what would happen there, and it came to pass. Through this gift we have the ability to help people and to prepare them for things that are ahead. Many times God has shown me things along this line that have blessed and helped individuals. We need this kind of manifestation today.

The Lord said to me, "If I give you a message for an individual, a church, or a pastor, and they don't accept it, you will not be responsible. They will be responsible. There will be ministers who don't accept it and will fall dead in the pulpit."

I say this with reluctance, but this actually happened in one place where I preached. Two weeks from the day that I closed the meeting, the pastor fell dead in the pulpit. When I left that church I left crying. I told the pastor in the next church where I went to hold a meeting, "That man will fall dead in the pulpit." And just a very short time after that he did. Why? Because he didn't accept the message that God gave me to give him from the Holy Spirit.

Some people think that we do not need a prophet's ministry in the New Testament dispensation since we all have the Holy Spirit. However, the Lord pointed out to me that in the days of the Old Testament, the laity did not have the Holy Ghost. The Holy Ghost came upon the priests, kings, and prophets to anoint them to stand in those offices. But even though the kings and priests had the Holy Ghost, they still went to the prophets for guidance. If one has the Holy Spirit, that doesn't mean he has the revelation gifts in operation.

As the Lord continued to speak with me concerning the prophet's ministry, He reminded me that just the day before the accident I had received a letter from a large church inviting me for a meeting. Although I had made no demands for salary, they had promised me a generous amount of money if I would come to their church. At that particular time I needed the money very much. If we are not careful, we will sometimes do things for convenience.

I had decided to write to this pastor and tell him I could come to his church. However, everytime I thought about it, I had a dead feeling in my spirit. Later I realized that this was the Holy Ghost cautioning me not to go. It was a stop sign that He had put there. The Lord didn't want me to go as the pastor would not have accepted my ministry. I would have been wasting my time.

As the Lord continued to speak with me, He said, "I am not going to lead you and guide you by a prophet's ministry. The inward witness is something that every believer can have. I am telling you not to go to that church."

The Lord then reminded me of an invitation I had received from a small church. This pastor had asked me to come to his church if the Lord ever led me to. I had almost forgotten about this invitation, but at different times while I was praying, that invitation would come to my mind. And when I would think about going to that church, I would get a good feeling, more or less a green light in my spirit—something urging me to go. The Lord told me that was an inward witness. We are not led, He said, by a prophet's ministry. We are led by the Holy Spirit, generally through an inward witness.

The prophet's ministry is used many times to confirm the leading that we already have. "As they ministered to the Lord, and fasted, the Holy Ghost said, Separate me Barnabas and Saul for the work whereunto I have called them" (Acts 13:2). Notice that they were not called that day to be missionaries or apostles to the Gentiles. They already had the calling. It was just confirmed. And we need this ministry just as much today as they needed it then.

One time I was praying with a pastor about a certain decision that he was to make. He hadn't told me exactly what he wanted prayer for. As we were praying together, I began to speak out a psalm which was a message to him. It told him what he had been thinking and what he was waiting on. This message repeated word for word what he had just told his wife. He had a witness in his heart, but he didn't know for certain. This message was the confirmation he needed. It lifted a great burden from him, for he was not sure of his way.

As the Lord sat there by my bed He said, "If you will learn to follow this inward witness, I will help you in all the affairs of your life. If my children will listen to me, I will make them wealthy. I am not opposed to their being rich, I am only opposed to their being covetous." I have learned to follow that inward witness, and it has been a great blessing to me in every area of life.

As Jesus finished His conversation with me He said, "Be faithful, fulfill your ministry, for the time is short." Then He got up from the chair and walked around the foot of the bed. He walked to the door, opened it, and stepped outside. Leaving the door slightly ajar, He walked on down the hall. I heard His footsteps fade away down the corridor, just as I had heard Him approaching nearly an hour and a half earlier.

8

The River of Praise

The Lord appeared to me again for the seventh time while I was conducting a meeting in Houston, Texas, in December, 1962. On the night of December 12, while preaching my message I was telling the people of how the Lord appeared to me in my first vision back in 1950. As I related some of the things that the Lord told me in that first vision, I began to see more clearly what He meant by some of those statements, and I saw where I had failed to obey Him completely.

Immediately I fell on my knees behind the pulpit. I began to cry and say, "Lord, forgive me. I have not obeyed You fully." As I knelt there I fell into a trance such as Peter did on the housetop, which we read about in the tenth chapter of Acts, when he had the vision of the sheet being let down from heaven by the four corners. By this method God led Peter to bring the Gentiles into the Kingdom of God.

While I was in this trance, I saw a beautiful flower garden. It seemed to be a square garden with a white picket fence around it which was overgrown with flowers. Climbing roses covered the fence in a solid mass so that it almost appeared to be a fence made entirely of flowers. Inside the garden was a mass of flowers in full bloom. An arbor covered with climbing flowers stood in the middle of the garden.

This sight was so glorious it is absolutely indescribable. There are no words which could tell of its beauty. Such an aroma went up from these flowers that the fragrance seemed to be multiplied a hundredfold, forming a cloud of incense.

I walked up to the garden from the east, and when I reached the gate Jesus was there to open it for me. He stretched out His right hand, and taking my right hand into His, He pulled me through the gate into the garden. Then with His left hand He closed the gate.

He took me down a walkway through the middle of the garden to the arbor. He drew me under the arbor where I saw two white marble seats, one on either side of the arbor. Jesus sat down and invited me to sit down on the marble seat on the south side of the arbor.

As I looked at Him I could see to the west of the garden. I asked, "What does this mean? What are all of these flowers? What do these represent? I have never seen any place like this in all of my life nor smelled any fragrance so magnificent!"

To the west I saw flowing into the garden what looked like a river. As I looked up this river it narrowed where it came into the garden. Then it seemed to become wider and wider, rising into the sky. It must have been fifty feet wide or more. The river seemed to be pouring tons of water into the garden.

Then the water changed and ceased to be water. It was people. Instead of a river of water it was a river of people. I saw men with high-top silk hats and long-tail coats, and women in evening gowns. I saw business men in smartly tailored suits. I saw laborers and housewives with their work clothes and aprons on. I saw people of all sorts—all of them singing praises as they flowed into the garden.

Then the Lord said to me, "These people that you see flowing like a river into this garden are what you call 'denominational people' or denominations other than the Full Gospel. In this day I am visiting hungry hearts everywhere. Wherever I find hearts that are open to Me, in whatever church they may be, I will visit them in this hour. I will also visit places that you never would have thought I would visit—not only what you call 'denominational churches' but I will also visit other religions where hearts are hungry and open to Me. I will bring them into a full salvation and into the baptism of the Holy Ghost. This river is all these people who will be called in these last days that will flow as one and will come together as one. The beautiful aroma of these flowers is the praise of these people ascending into heaven, even as the incense of old ascended unto Me."

Then the Lord said to me, "You must play a part in this. You will work with these people in the various denominations. You will minister to Full Gospel people to help them to be prepared for my coming. I will show you how and what to do."

Then He took my hand, lifted me up, and walked with me back to the gate. He opened it with His left hand, still holding my right hand in His. I went through the gate and then He closed it behind me. As I stood just outside the gate, the vision disappeared.

I came to myself and realized that I was on my face behind the pulpit. I arose and told the people what I had seen, and it blessed and inspired all of us.

We have seen this vision come to pass to some extent since 1962, but we have not seen the fullness of it yet. That river is still flowing. There are many yet that will come to this river of God and shall drink of it, and shall walk in the fullness of the spirit. They will come from every church and from every country. And we are seeing this fulfilled and will continue to see it fulfilled in the days that are just before us.

9

The Angel's Message

The eighth time I saw the Lord, or the next "divinely granted appearance," as the AMPLIFIED BIBLE says, that I had was in August, 1963. It was primarily for my own benefit; however, it does involve the ministry and for this reason I shall relate it here.

At this time we were in an eight-week series of meetings, and during the last three weeks we set aside two nights a week in which there was no preaching. We just spent our time praying together as believers. I had told the people that there would be no sermon but only prayer on those nights, and if they were not coming to pray not to plan to come to the services. Yet the crowds were as large on those nights as they were on the other nights.

One night as we were all interceding in prayer, I was kneeling on the platform when suddenly Jesus appeared before me. Again, an angel stood about three feet behind Him. This angel was quite tall; he must have been seven feet tall or more.

Jesus began to talk to me about my ministry. Just a short time before this, my wife had written me concerning my sister who had just been told by the doctors that she had cancer of the bladder. I had been praying for my sister and interceding for her that night just before the Lord appeared to me. He said, "Your sister will live and not die. There is no danger of immediate death." He said that she would live at least another five years. And she did. When she died after five years exactly, she did not die from the condition that existed at that time. Her death was caused by something else.

After the Lord told me that my sister would live, then every time I looked up at the angel, he looked at me as if he was going to say something. But then I would look back to Jesus and the angel wouldn't say anything. Finally I said to the Lord, "Who is this angel and what does he represent?"

"He has a message for you," the Lord said.

"But Lord, You are here. Why can't You deliver the message?" After all, I wanted to be Scriptural. The Holy Spirit is to be our guide. He is the one that is to give us guidance as well as the Word of God. So I said, "You know that I am a real stickler for the Word."

Jesus said to me, "Didn't you ever read in the Bible where an angel of the Lord came and awakened Peter when he was in jail, and in answer to prayer led him out of jail? Don't you remember that the angel of the Lord appeared to Philip, and gave him directions after that great city-wide meeting in Samaria, telling him to go down by the way of Gaza? And there, you will remember, the Ethiopian eunuch was converted to Christianity and carried the gospel back to Ethiopia.

"Don't you remember that the angel of the Lord appeared to Paul when he was on board the ship on his way to Rome to appeal his case before Caesar? A storm had arisen and all the merchandise on the ship had been thrown overboard in an attempt to save the vessel and its passengers. But all hope that they should be saved was gone. Then Paul stood and said, '. . . I exhort you to be of good cheer: for there shall be no loss of any man's life among you, but of the ship. For there stood by me this night the angel of God, whose I am, and whom I serve, Saying, Fear not, Paul; thou must be brought before Caesar: and, lo, God hath given thee all them that sail with thee'" (Acts 27:22-24).

Then the Lord said, "Didn't the angel give Paul direction? Didn't he have a message for Paul?"

The Lord reminded me of the time when Paul was praying in the temple in Jerusalem and fell into a trance and saw Jesus who told him, ". . . Make haste, and get thee quickly out of Jerusalem . . ." (Acts 22:18). Then after Paul was arrested, before appealing his case to Caesar, the Lord appeared to him one night in jail in Jerusalem and told him not to be afraid, that he was to bear witness of His name before the kings and authorities.

So we see that although Jesus had appeared to Paul and had given him words of comfort and direction, the angel of the Lord had also appeared to him and had given him direction.

Seeing this, then, I said to the Lord, "All right, Lord, now I understand." Then I looked to the angel and said, "What is it that you have to say to me?"

"I am sent from God to tell you that the money will come by October, and you will have $4,000 so you can set up your own office and make your own tapes. Other money will come and you will handle it all yourself. I do not want you to be controlled by someone else. I will speak to you and direct you in your ministry. You will be the head of it—not someone else. Not only will you have this $4,000 in three months' time, but other money will come also, for my angels are at work now to cause the money to come."

I said, "What do you mean, 'your angels'?"

He said, "I am head over a number of angels."

In teaching me about angels, the Lord had also pointed out the Scripture, "Are they not all ministering spirits, sent forth to minister for them who shall be heirs of salvation" (Hebrews 1:14)?

I had always thought that this verse said, ". . . minister to them who shall be heirs of salvation." But the Word says ". . . minister for them . . ." The word "minister" used here carries the thought of "to wait on" or "to serve." For instance, when you go into a restaurant, a waitress comes to minister to you, to wait on you, or to serve you. In other words, she waits for your order.

The Lord said to me, "Angels are ministering spirits who are sent to minister, not just to one, but for all those who are heirs of salvation."

Someone might ask, "Well, why haven't they done anything then?" They are waiting on you to give them the order, just as the waitress cannot do anything for you until you give her the order.

After the angel delivered his message to me the Lord said, "Now respond to him." I remembered then that in a previous vision the Lord had told me that my angel would appear to me. "My angel?" I had said.

"Yes," He said. "You don't lose your angel just because you grow up."

Just as the angel had said, by October $4,000 had come in and we were able to establish our office. We are able to do the work of God and not be under bondage to anybody. I have learned now to say, "Go, ministering spirit, and cause the needed money to come in."

I praise God that He will direct us and guide us today, even by visions when necessary, not as we might will but as He wills!

Also by Kenneth Hagin

Authority of the Believer
Seven Vital Steps to Receiving the Holy Spirit
Right and Wrong Thinking
What Faith Is
How to Turn Your Faith Loose
Three Volume Series Dealing With Demons:
> Volume 1: The Origin and Operation of Demons
> Volume 2: Demons and How to Deal With Them
> Volume 3: Ministering to the Oppressed

Prayer Secrets
Redeemed From Poverty, Sickness and Death
The Ministry of the Prophet
The Key to Scriptural Healing
Why Every Believer Should Speak in Tongues
How You Can Know the Will of God
The Interceding Christian
The Real Faith
Healing Belongs to Us
The Gift of Prophecy
The Present Day Ministry of Jesus Christ
Praying to Get Results
Bible Prayer Study Course
Bible Faith Study Course
The Holy Spirit and His Gifts

*These books are available from your
book store, or you may write to:*

Kenneth E. Hagin Evangelistic Association, Inc.
P.O. Box 50126
Tulsa, Oklahoma 74150